HAMLETICS

THE ITALIAN LIST

Massimo Cacciari

Hamletics

SHAKESPEARE, KAFKA, BECKETT

Translated by Matteo Mandarini

LONDON NEW YORK CALCUTTA

This book has been translated thanks to a translation grant awarded by the Italian Ministry of Foreign Affairs and International Cooperation.

Questo libro è stato tradotto grazie a un contributo alla traduzione assegnato dal Ministero degli Affari Esteri e della Cooperazione Internazionale italiano.

Seagull Books, 2023

First published in Italian as *Hamletica*
© 2009 Adelphi Edizioni s.p.a. Milan

First published in English translation by Seagull Books, 2023
English translation © Matteo Mandarini, 2023

ISBN 978 1 80309 266 9

British Library Cataloguing-in-Publication Data
A catalogue record for this book is available from the British Library

Typeset by Seagull Books, Calcutta, India
Printed and bound by Hyam Enterprises, India

CONTENTS

The Aporias of Action

The work of Massimo Cacciari, one of Italy's foremost philosophers of the last half century, can often appear daunting and abstruse, if not downright obscure. This is—at least in some ways—a misprision, for unlike much academic philosophy, Cacciari does not work with the technical jargon of a tradition, so much as the sedimented conceptual, cultural and semantic richness of language itself; albeit a language that is resonating with multiple, principally European philosophical traditions. There is much Nietzsche, much Heidegger and, in some ways, much Freud in his work, in the sense of a penetrating attentiveness to language, its uses contemporary and ancient; an active, living philological sensibility that Cacciari draws upon, deploys and abides within but in such a way as to show that such reverberating connotations are always active, whether we are aware of them or not. Cacciari's prose is rich and allusive, but—in this work at least—it does not always demand a specific technical knowledge, protectively safeguarded by those 'in the know'. To some extent, the text itself can be said to provide its own key, the key to the pursuance of thinking, of language itself as sense-vehicle: the vehicle itself, the form itself, is the content; the content, the form— and yet one that is irreducible to 'mere' words. Presupposed is always an absence, an unspoken pre-propositional 'condition' upon which concrete linguistic expressions and thought itself weave themselves. As Cacciari writes elsewhere: 'the manifestation of a dimension that does not transcend common language, but is riveted to it, immanent to every weft, foreign to the quotidian logic of contradiction, foreign to the daily principle of non-contradiction.'[1] The 'condition' is not transcendental, since it is 'no-thing' (in the hyphenated forms he's famous for, highlighting the component elements of meaning to what is normally conceived as a single word); it is that no-thing that permits language, thought and—as we shall see—acting to perform themselves, interminably.

We can say that in *Hamletics*, many of the theoretical resources martialled are immanent to the literary and dramatic texts under consideration. That is not to deny that there are richly resonant, semantic, lexical and conceptual elements from a host of disciplinary fields: most notably philosophical, theological, poetic, juridical; but whereas most philosophical writing is situated squarely *within* a tradition and is *of* it, the work of Cacciari—and this book in particular—is interstitial and, as such, works contrapuntally. At the heart of his work is what we might call a negative space, which is not a space of dialectical negation, but one that logically precedes all division, distinction, opposition, and is at work necessarily in all 'subsequent' (not in a temporal sense) differentiations and, yet positively exists only in those oppositions, those distinctions that it permits but which it always escapes. As we shall see, this negative space might also be framed as the pure possible, or the 'im-possible'.

Having said all this, some reference to the complex theoretical debates out of which Cacciari has woven his own idiosyncratic metaphysical meditations might be useful, especially to readers previously unacquainted with his work—although such an effort will necessarily be somewhat cursory and superficial. Cacciari's thought, at least since the 1960s, sets itself against a certain reading of German

---

1 Massimo Cacciari, *Icone della legge* (Milan: Adelphi, 1986), p. 89.

idealism. I won't engage with the details of his critique, which occupied Cacciari since the 1960s and that is presupposed in all his subsequent work. But to grasp the critique's basic coordinates it is helpful to understand the idealist image of thought against which it pits itself. As the Italian Marxist philosopher Nicola Badaloni observed:

> The logical core of idealist philosophy can be grasped in the relationship that it founds between thinking and doing. Thinking again on the meaning of the Hegelian system, [Benedetto] Croce wrote: 'With Hegel one achieved the awareness that man is his history, history is the one reality, history *that is made as freedom* and is *thought as necessity*; which is no longer that capricious sequence of events of reason, but is instead the actualization of reason that is only called irrational when it disdains and fails to recognize itself in history.' The freedom-necessity relationship is thus understood by Croce in the sense of thought, 'rendered transparent in the light of the true', restoring the material offered by practice, impressing upon it the seal of necessity.[2]

It is this 'logical core'—Reason as the source of the objective world and of subjective action—that Cacciari sets himself against; and he does so, not in favour of the irrational, but in contrast with what he sees as the complacent standpoint of bourgeois thought, which presumes to reach a point of pacific settlement between reason and history, thought and action, the economy and the political.[3]

---

2 Nicola Badaloni, *Marxismo come storicismo* (Milan: Feltrinelli, 1975[1962]), p. 7.
3 On this last opposition, see Cacciari's *The Labour of Spirit*, forthcoming from Seagull Books.

Badaloni writes: 'The hard lesson that we have inherited from [the Marxist] tradition lies precisely in not permitting thought to separate itself from the wave of the real in its movement.'[4] Cacciari's account distances itself resolutely from such a position.[5] For him, the 'real movement' is rather the chain of events, the meaningless '[c]ompactness, density of this world'[6] that renders authentic action—action that *decides*—impossible. Cacciari sees such a Marxian perspective, the one Badaloni ascribes to Gramsci for instance, as failing to escape the pacific account provided by German idealism, at whose core lies the utopian moment of resolved conflict, which is characteristic of the bourgeoisie in its ascendency.

Let us start at the beginning—and the beginning raises the question of commencement, of knowledge as well as of action. What does it mean to act? What does it mean to know? If all action *is*, if it has an intrinsic relation to *being*, it must also somehow *know* the realm of existence within which it takes place—i.e. the unfolding course of events. Cacciari's own later work has set out from the question of beginning, from commencement, from the initiation of knowledge, placing his own thinking within the long history of the history of philosophy and onto-theological questions of beginning.[7] But let us proceed in some sort of order. We could begin in several different

---

4 Badaloni, *Marxismo come storicismo*, p. 36–37.

5 And from such an account of Marxism. Cacciari's relationship to Marxism is a complex one, which we cannot go into here. An important piece—perhaps one that can be considered an example of Cacciari's own *Kehre*—on his relationship to this question, can be found in English translation: 'Confrontation with Heidegger' (Timothy S. Murphy trans.), *Genre* 43(3–4) (2010): 353–68.

6 In this volume, p. 46.

7 See especially what is arguably his most ambitious work, the 700-page *Dell'Inizio* [On the beginning] (Milan: Adelphi, 1990).

places, with Parmenides and the two paths, of day and night, truth and oblivion. Or we could begin with Plato and the need to hold on to thoughts that do not undermine themselves, as they do in the empirical world where everything is in-becoming and thus always what it is and what it is not, in the arising and cessation of things. Leaping forward almost two millennia, we might begin with Descartes and the demand that we have something to hold onto, something which we cannot doubt as a steady foundation for knowledge, about which we cannot be deceived. We shall instead begin with Germany, with the debates in post-Kantian philosophy—if somewhat briskly.

If knowledge can be understood as justified true belief, it must presuppose something that is given without further grounding, for all grounds of knowledge would themselves call, in turn, for knowledge of those grounds—and so on *ad infinitum*. But this would, as such, undermine the very search for justification, thus making knowledge (as justified true belief) impossible. This sceptical conclusion could only be escaped if there were to be an unconditioned ground, grasped or experienced immediately, presupposed in all knowing. In the paradoxical formulation of some post-Kantian German Romantics, this absolute 'not-knowing' was 'associated with the idea of Being—not as something that can be reduced to a condition of knowability, but certainly as something that must be thought of as the foundation of these conditions';[8] famously, German Romanticism would find in 'feeling' a point of access, a revelation or non-discursive manifestation of such an unconditioned. It is this pre-conceptual moment that sets the stage for what Cacciari will go on to call the Presupposition, or the Impossible or—at one and the same time—the 'pure possible',[9] understood as what exists prior to any division, any

---

8 Manfred Frank, *The Philosophical Foundations of German Romanticism* (Elizabeth Millán-Zaibert trans.) (Albany, NY: SUNY Press), p. 57—but see the whole of Frank's third lecture.

9 Cacciari, *Icone della legge*, p. 104.

distinction or differentiation. It is this zone of indiscernibility that is at the philosophical heart of Cacciari's reflections, and is investigated in different registers—whether these be strictly philosophical, aesthetic, juridical, ethical, etc. It is this 'space' that reveals itself in the aporias of action that are on display in Cacciari's reflections on Shakespeare, Kafka and Beckett in this text.

All action rests upon a decision, a cut or separation (from the Latin de-, 'off', and caedere, 'to cut') within the course of the empirical network of events that is the world; but decision itself, as that which 'founds' a course of action through a cut in the course of historical time, is itself unfounded and so can never truly begin. For decision takes place alongside historical time and, hence, the 'iron cage' of the chain of events. A decision to act is made which cuts into a chain of events that determines the subject of decision and escapes that subject of action on all sides, back into times immemorial and forward into the not-yet; as such, action is commanded, determined and thus is im-possible, for only that which is within the empirical chain of being is 'possible' (as Kant had shown in the *Critique of Pure Reason*). As Cacciari noted many years ago:

> The concept of *Freiheit* [freedom] has, in the entire tradition of western metaphysics, meant the *opposite* of acting *within being-there*. It has always meant *extricating* oneself from being-there, posing the possibility of going-beyond. *Freiheit* has always had an inseparable affinity with the concept of substance and the in-itself. *Freiheit* is the unrealization of the world, existing ecstasy *for* substance—an instrument for the comprehension of the in-itself. If there is *Freiheit* there is no *possibility* of action. *A priori* the world of *operari* [work, labour] and the idea of *Freiheit* exclude one another.[10]

10 Massimo Cacciari, 'Pensiero negativo e razionalizzazione. Problemi e funzione della critica al sistema dialettico' in *Pensiero negativo e razionalizzazione* (Venice: Marsilio, 1977), p. 43.

Action can only take place within the world; but the world is the world of the causal determination of events; thus, action is ever-always caught within the iron cage. In the world, one is decided not decider, and so cannot found or initiate, which is the very condition of decision. De-cision—as Cacciari writes to foreground its etymology and conceptual composition—is the im-possible shadow that accompanies action within the world; it is the pure possible which, once it shows itself, is captured at the same as it unsettles any ease or comfort or pacific realization. De-cision is that without which one cannot distinguish action from the mere observable chain of phenomena of the natural or technical world. It is this tension, this aporetic nature of action that underpins the analyses that Cacciari provides in this brief but dense text.

We must ask, in conclusion: why explore these issues through the work of two dramatists, William Shakespeare and Samuel Beckett, and the novels, stories and aphorisms of Franz Kafka? One can begin to explore this question by returning, again, to the device of etymology. The ancient Greek word for drama, *Drân*, means 'to do', 'to act', 'to perform': it is the very possibility of acting that is explored in the theatrical space, which stages the possibilities (and im-possibilities) of acting. One can open this book on any page and find the aporias of action revealed, as in the discussion of Beckett's *Waiting for Godot*:

> What acting, what *drama* corresponds to the 'impression of existing'? 'Nothing to be done' are its first words. From the representation of action par excellence, the *drama* has become expression of being always and only 'potentially'. Up to relinquishing even of this 'waiting' for the 'act'. Vladimir is the *persona* of the first moment of this metamorphosis.

Might we not see the stage as mimicking the iron cage, wherein action happens, where acting performs its ineffectuality in the world while revealing also acting to be the pure possible—*in*-action as a performance of its potential that opens vistas irreducible to the staging that aims to contain it? And is this not Kafka's very problem, the in-decision that always calls for action at the same time as marking the pure potential, always unrealized but not for that reason any less 'real' of the acting itself; in-consequential but always infinitely reproposed? To draw on a Wittgensteinian distinction dear to Cacciari, the stage and the parable don't say but show the parabolas of the aporias of action.

Translator's Acknowledgements

Thanks to Alberto Toscano for his meticulous editorial suggestions and for the numerous insights that made their way into the notes. Thanks also to S. K. for accompanying me in the exploration of the aporias of action.

Author's Note

The themes of this tripartite essay were developed, extemporaneously, in separate lessons and conferences over the course of several years. Reflecting upon them, I glimpsed, among the authors and works that lie at the heart of this book, unexpected and unsettling relations that I have sought to clarify and flesh out. The path goes from the 'to do', from an acting [*agire*] that still feels able to 'decide'—albeit in Hamlet's universal *insecuritas*—to K.'s bewildered, *di-verted* [*s-viato*] acting in *The Castle*, arriving at the paradoxical image of the untranscendability of his own 'in-completion', and lastly to the *spent* and thus inexhaustible character of Beckett. I have appended to this work a brief piece, with minor amendments from its earlier publication in *Humanitas* (March–April 2000—with thanks to the journal's editor Ilario Bertoletti), which I think will help the comprehension of the pages dedicated to Kafka.

The Spectre of Action

'To be or not to be . . .'—the problem lies in how this is to be translated. Does being not mean *to do*? Is not the very Supreme Being the perfect identity of will and power? It was called *actuositas* by that 'furious' southerner who caused so much scandal in Albion less than two decades before Hamlet's appearance.[1] Being is will, but a will that accomplishes what it wants. Principle,[2] *arché* of movement, certainly, but in no way separate; it is immanent to the universal mobility of entities. Each entity subsists only insofar as it is energy exhibiting the *actuositas* of Being, '"mover" and "agitator of the universe"',[3] 'smithy of the world', 'internal artificer',[4] power and act are at the Beginning co-implicated, while they become 'specified' in particular entities. The entity is inasmuch as it is a 'simulacrum' of that Principle which is everything in everything and which ceaselessly 'agitates' everything. This was a vision of the fecundity of Being of

---

1 The reference is to Giordano Bruno—born in Nola, a province of Naples—and specifically to his *Eroici furori* [Heroic furies] (1585). [Trans.]
2 In Italian, *principio* combines principle, principal and beginning. All these senses should be born in mind, as in the Greek *archē*. [Trans.]
3 Giordano Bruno, *Cause, Principle and Unity, and Writings on Magic* (Richard J. Blackwell and Robert de Lucca trans and eds) (Cambridge: Cambridge University Press, 1998), p. 38.
4 Bruno, *Cause, Principle and Unity*, p. 38.

which the Nolan[5] was enthusiastic. He had sown so many fruitful seeds in Elizabethan England and had 'decided', so as not to renounce them, to die at the stake a few years after the Prince of Denmark was born in the mind of Shakespeare.[6]

'To do or not to do . . .'—how can one not-do if the Principle itself is an *inter-esse*,[7] a factor and participant in universal animation? But *how* can one do? This is the problem. To do is said in many ways. In the Beginning, will—to decide to do—and the completion of the work are One; but in the mind of this finite existence? in the power of his *hand*? An abyss appears to open between the Supreme Being and its simulacrum! This is a very vague similarity rather than an authentic analogy. For one reason above all: to act [*operare*] 'down here' can appear so difficult and tormenting as to induce us or 'seduce us' to not-do, to decide to 'secede' from doing. This is the new drama: no longer a representation of action, but a question concerning its nature, a doubt concerning its necessity. *Drân*, the tragic verb par excellence, the acting-that-decides, resolute till the end, whether it be a happy accomplishment or a shipwreck, has become a problem, a

---

5 Originating from the town of Nola in the province of Naples. 'Nolan' is often is used, with the definite article, as another name for Bruno. [Trans.]
6 Leaving aside the issue of the 'first Hamlet' and its author, it is beyond doubt that Shakespeare had begun thinking of *Hamlet* well before the version of the play published in the 1604–5 edition (see Alessandro Serpieri, 'Il mistero del primo Amleto' in William Shakespeare, *Il primo Amleto* [A. Serpieri trans. and ed.] [Venice: Marsilio, 1997]). See Gilberto Sacerdoti's *Sacrificio e sovranità*: *Teologia e politica nell'Europa di Shakespeare e Bruno* (Macerata: Quodlibet, 2016) for a notable contribution on the relations between Elizabethan literary and philosophical culture and Bruno's Italian works, in light of the political and religious events of the period.
7 *Inter-esse* is one of many Cacciari's wordplays. In this case, he draws upon the two Latinate lexical elements of 'between' and 'to be'. *Interesse* in Italian also means interest, as in 'of interest to' or 'in the interests of'. [Trans.]

THE SPECTRE OF ACTION

question.[8] The protagonist does not act without doubting the sense of his acting. His drama becomes an interrogation of the *drân*. Each time his mind, in 'imitation' of the Principle, wants to express itself as effective power, each time it wants to realize itself, it is thrown back onto its pure being-possible. But if being is will-to-power inasmuch as it is a capacity to command and to order, pure being-possible will be the 'name' of non-being or of the illusion of being. *To do* means, according to its very etymology, ordering power (it is the fatal root **dhe: e-the-ka, fe-ci*, so have I disposed, so have I done); 'not to do' is a ghostly condition.

Nevertheless, the ghost is not simply 'not to be'. It cannot act, certainly, but it appears. It demands to be *represented*, to have a *stand-in*. But what does such a claim mean? To want a second self? To want to re-present itself? But how could the 'representative' coincide with the represented? These are aporias of the very idea of representation. Insurmountable aporias of 'political theatre'.[9]

They are aporias that the ghost would like to ignore. He is the *bearer of the past*; on this basis he makes a claim on the present. He

---

8 The editors of the Norton Critical Edition of Aristotle's *Poetics* point out that the 'word *drama* (a thing done) is derived from *drân* (to do)' (Aristotle, *Poetics* [Michelle Zerba and David Gorman trans and eds] [New York: Norton & Company, 2018], p. 5n1). See also the French collection of Cacciari's writings on this theme: *Drân: Meridiens de la decisión dans la pensée contemporaine* (Michel Valensi trans.) (París: L'Éclat, 1991). [Trans.]

9 On the problem of 'representation' in general, see Hasso Hoffmann's formidable work, *Rappresentanza—rappresentazione: Parola e concetto dall'antichità all'Ottocento* (C. Tomassi trans.) (Milan: Giuffrè, 2007) [Italian translation of *Repräsentation: Studien zur Wort- und Begriffsgeschichte von der Antike bis ins 19. Jahrhundert* (Berlin: Duncker und Humblot, 1974)]. It ranges across the history of the term, from the theological to the juridical dimension where, strangely, it fails to engage with great Elizabethan drama and baroque theatre.

is the ghost of the lineage to which the son belongs inexorably. The ghost does not ask to be 'redeemed' but to be 'continued'—that his 'uncompleted' actions be brought to completion by those who survive him. Only in this way could the past 'rest'. What is *done* produces the inextricable net of conditions into which current doing is 'thrown'. It is impossible for the past to 'leave in peace' since its acts exist in the present, acting like an energy that prevents the latter from being unconditionally 'free'. Consumed action *consumes*. The past is so immanent to *his* being-present that it must assume his very name: Hamlet.

Hence this name is a *historic* figure—and Carl Schmitt is right to seek out all its references to the events of the time, investigating its *Sitz-im-Leben*[10] in the period of religious and political conflicts between Elizabeth and James.[11] The essence of Hamlet is historical because he exists as a figure inasmuch as he is essentially conditioned by the drama of *facts*, 'chained' to the set of irrevocable links from which every decision issues.[12] To decide—and the will to act cannot

---

10 Setting or place in life—a formula employed in Biblical criticism to refer to the context and circumstances in the life of a community for a particular scene, parable or story. [Trans.]

11 Carl Schmitt, *Hamlet or Hecuba: The Intrusion of Time into the Play* (David Pan and Jennifer R. Rust trans) (New York: Telos Press, 2009). More broadly on the 'political' Shakespeare, see Ekkehart Krippendorff, *Shakespeare politico: Drammi storici, drammi romani, tragedie* (Rome: Fazi, 2005) [the Italian translation by Robin Benatti and Francesca Materzanini of *Politik in Shakespeares Dramen: Historien, Römerdramen, Tragödien* (Frankfurt: Suhrkamp, 1992)].

12 The importance assumed in the economy of the play by apparently superfluous references to political events stems from this. 'What takes place without the theatre, what the spectator does not see, but must imagine for himself, is like a background, in front of which the acting figures move. Your large and simple prospect of the fleet and Norway will very much improve

be otherwise conceived—cannot 'liberate' from the prison of the already-done. One must discover one's route within it, necessarily 'compromising oneself' with it. For prison has 'many confines, wards, and dungeons' (2.2 in the First Folio [1623]).[13] This prison is a labyrinth, the 'home' of all disguises, hypocrisy and lies. But only here does *doing* appear possible.

The world of the court, of royalty that Rosencrantz described, where all solitude is denied, where every part is subordinated to the Whole, this 'total institution' is the image of the prison within which the drama of historical existence unfolds. Every entity 'is bound' insofar as it is an element in the chain; it *closes* itself and what is other than itself. Each decision is produced based on what has been decided and fastens its own link with those that are to-come. But this means that we are not the 'subjects' who have power over the origin and the end. The decision is assumed on the basis and in-the-face-of *facts* that we will never truly know, since we did not accomplish them and given that their outcome will depend upon the interweaving of further and *other* actions, which we cannot foresee. The knowledge that is given to historical existence consists in knowing that its doing will never be able to shed light on what it does, that no certain relation links thought and plan to the product of acting. 'Our wills and fates do so contrary run / That our devices still are overthrown;

---

the piece: if this were altogether taken from it, we should have but a family-scene remaining; and the great idea, that here a kingly house by internal crimes and incongruities goes down to ruin, would not be presented with its proper dignity.' J. W. Goethe, *Wilhelm Meister's Apprenticeship and Travels*, VOL. 1 (Thomas Carlyle trans.) (New York: A. L. Burt, 1839), BOOK 5, CHAP. 5, p. 269.

13 From this point onwards, all references to *Hamlet* are to the Second Quarto (1604/05) version, unless otherwise stated.

/ Our thoughts are ours, their ends none of our own' (3.2).[14] This is the Shakespearean 'mourning scene,' against which one should project Vico's 'new science'.

Facts present themselves to Hamlet in their most imposing and oppressive fashion, displaying the 'same frown' with which he conducted his battles and overthrew his enemies. His voice is that of Hercules, 'in complete steel' (1.4), which demands the ultimate *judgement*: life or death, kill or be killed, enemy or friend. The ghost demands a pure decision. But what sort of decision is it that is imposed? Moreover, is this not a paradoxical figure, the imposing one of the King who continues to assert his indisputable sovereignty in the shape of a ghost? Here is a larva, an illusory King who wishes obsessively to 'recur'. The nightmare of the already-done atop of historical existence. The sovereignty of the past, which pretends to

---

14 The great tragic characters '*are* what they will and accomplish'. G. W. F. Hegel, *Aesthetics: Lectures on Fine Art*, VOL. 2 (T. M. Knox trans.) (Oxford: Oxford University Press, 1975), p. 1214. Acting [*agire*], which belongs to them entirely, represents fate itself. Yet the character's nature clashes with the end he seeks to accomplish. What he is called to do has become 'cleaved' from the 'substance of his own individuality'. *Hamlet* represents the full awareness of the difference between modern and ancient drama. Before Hegel, Schelling had already understood this in *The Philosophy of Art* (1802–3). Character is erected to replace ancient fate: he does, he decides. But what the subject performs is split from its most intimate content. The subject 'alienates' itself fatally in pursuing what it feels called to. *Nemesis* is the name that Schelling gives to this fatal concatenation of facts, due to which subjective intention loses itself in the world. *Facts* is what they all are beyond doubt and not manifestations of Ananke. All are determined by historical energies and historical wills, but their succession and results constitute a network that constantly transcends the will, projects, and the expectations of 'free' subjectivity.

command current doing; the past that refuses to set. Hamlet has Hamm's curse in *Endgame* stuck in his craw: 'Accursed progenitor!';[15] the more he suffocates it by repeatedly extolling the heroic past ('the front of Jove himself; / An eye like Mars, to threaten and command; / A station like the herald Mercury / New lighted on a heaven-kissing hill: / A combination and a form indeed / Where every god did seem to set his seal / To give the world the assurance of a man' [3.4]), the more muffled it resounds at the base of each of his words.

The more historical existence detests its *debt*, its not-having the 'key' to the past upon which it nevertheless rests, the more it becomes aware of the burden of having to respond to it. The idolatrous respect for history, as Nietzsche said in his *Untimely Meditations*, condemns one to the loss of the courage to make it. But it is not the apparent idolatry for his father that blocks Hamlet, nor the 'guilt' of never being able to fully reply to his call. Hamlet doubts he will be able to decide because he knows he is essentially ignorant of the past, which nevertheless binds each decision, precisely at the time that his father reveals it to him. It is fate that at that moment the question should arise: *who* calls? On what foundations does the demand stand? And which foundation, which 'grounds' can judge my actions to be 'responsible'? This is where the crisis strikes. The chain of actions impedes a priori all *apatheia*. Not even Horatio, whose philosophy Hamlet laughs at bitterly, is the stoic 'spectator'; he is rather the 'political' stoic who takes part in the tragic 'game' and is able to discover a potential majesty in his friend. Everyone 'unfolds' the chain of actions, whether as Horatio, as warrior or as courtier. And there are those who, as we shall see, do so as victims. But upon these

---

15 In this wa,y Hamm also has stuck in his craw the name Ham-let. See Nadia Fusini, *La passione dell'origine: Studi sul tragico shakespeariano e il romanzesco moderno* (Bari: Dedalo, 1981), especially Part 3.

personae falls a sinister light as soon as a 'prisoner', 'on waking', no matter how, interrogates themselves on the link between, on the one hand, the freedom to decide that they lay claim to, and, on the other, the necessary 'obedience' to the universe of facts and the links that condition and determine us on every side. The 'sureness' with which those *personae* intervened in the theatre of the world disappears at a stroke: the noble warrior rather resembles the adventurer that has gathered around himself a 'list of lawless resolutes' (1.1) (but is this not how the Romuluses act, all the true 'founders'?); the code of honour of the ancient courtier falls to the ground, corroded by hypocrisy and lies, in the same way that the symbol of majesty falls from Claudius' hands. The old masks no longer serve to protect. The 'question' has torn them asunder.

While the past imposes itself upon us and we continue to deploy its language, transforming it 'naturally' with mere speech; while our acting 'imitates' its codes, we can feel 'at home' even in wars and amid the harshest lacerations; but when one grasps the full burden of the past, when the 'responsibility' for it is borne and, at the same time, doubt emerges as to its meaning and to the foundation of its 'call', then nothing follows its course any more, everything must be re-ordered. The world is not 'out of joint' because of this or that crime (which have and will always take place, as the 'play within a play' demonstrates: that attempt to relive the royal murder, which cannot convince in relation to the action to be carried out here-and-now), but because the crime itself has become *próblema. Because acting itself has become one.* Are the orders that determined its different forms necessary? And if they are not, are they still legitimate? How can one obey them if I cannot but doubt them? And how can I overcome them if I doubt them? How can one *join* the gravitational force of the *fact* to the will to assert oneself as subject of a new order?

In what order is one to re-place the world whose joints appear to dissolve? In the old order? But it is precisely the old order that led to the present dissolution. A new order, then? But this will never happen without a radical *decision*—which is inconceivable if doing is always *thrown* into the web of facts. If Hamlet obeys Hamlet-King, he will only be able to reproduce the 'order' of catastrophe; but if he refuses to obey, in the name of what aims, on the 'ground' of which values will he act? Only a new god could justify the missing Father cult—and the absence of the former is a thousand times more deafening than the implacable thundering of the latter. But it is indeed an absence—whereas the ghost of the father is imperiously *real*[16] (the reality of *inactuositas* itself, absurd, paradoxical, 'new' reality), just as all the other parts of the web in which Hamlet struggles are real too.

Blessed, then, the times when our acting believed itself to reflect firmly established orders? Nobody in the play states this. But certainly, damned be those times in which order appears broken and nobody knows how to make-arrange [*farne-disporne*] a new one—in which a will to 'liberate' oneself from the past arises, and this will finds neither word nor foundation. Damned be the times in which we are born *as-if* we could make-order [*fare-ordinare*], whereas our acting is but in-decision, between the *fact* interrogated and called into doubt, and those ends of the present agitation and acting to which only 'a divinity' (5.2) could give form.

To act is necessary. Once everyone is on board. Not even death can represent a definite end of the 'game', for as Hamlet-King demonstrates, it too is condemned to appear. There is no 'happy' death, no 'good death'. Our actions do not terminate with death. On the one hand, the end is already in the beginning; on the other, it continues always. Beckett will restate this; Leopardi had already said it: the

---

16 *Reale* in Italian can mean 'real' or 'royal'. [Trans.]

souffrance of existing is as necessary as it is 'unlaudable'. Hamlet affirms it in the doubt that dominates his famous monologue: how can one truly think of ceasing to live, which is to say, to cease dying? Is death the 'consummation / Devoutly to be wish'd'?[17] Here one encounters the utmost difficulty, 'the rub'; here the decisive match is played out. Since we cannot remove the anguish of this something beyond death, the 'undiscover'd country' (3.1), we cannot even be certain of ending. But in this way the doubt concerning the radical incompleteness of existence informs each action. If that living that is dying does not end, no work within it can be said 'surely' to be accomplished. The ontological *insecuritas* concerning the ultimate end corrupts all resoluteness. Doubt and anguish do not, then, concern the 'something' beyond death, but the fact that this might reveal itself to be mere appearance, that life knows not how to truly die, *to decide*, in each instance, its own completion.

One dies badly, like a dog, when *one* dies. But will death, *verbum agentis*, not only be for those who have known how to *decide*, whereas for others, the either/or will ring *krepieren oder krepieren* ('to croak or to croak'), *out-out*, as Adorno wrote concerning two 'seeming deaths' of some of Beckett's characters?[18] This is the doubt

---

17 Hamlet's question is central to Schopenhauer's *World as Will and Representation*: 'Now if suicide really offered this [absolute non-being] [. . .] then it would be the clear choice, a highly desirable completion [*Vollendung*] ("a consummation devoutly to be wish'd"). But there is something in us telling us that it is not so; this is not the end, death is not an absolute termination [*keine absolute Vernichtung*].' Arthur Schopenhauer, *The World as Will and Representation*, VOL. 1 (Judith Norman, Alastair Welchman and Christopher Janaway trans and eds) (Cambridge: Cambridge University Press, 2010), pp. 350–51.

18 Theodor W. Adorno, 'Trying to Understand *Endgame*' in *Notes to Literature*, VOL. 1 (Shierry Weber Nicholsen trans.) (New York: Columbia University Press, 1992), p. 267.

that causes Hamlet such anguish: are those who lived badly destined to die badly? How will those who have been unable to complete their acts be able to complete their lives? What has not been decided, 'resolved', will necessarily continue to survive, chained to the web of causes and effects that is the universal law of *souffrance*. The undecided, then, are untouched by true death, or even true dream, but must continue to act, to 'grunt and sweat', although perhaps in other forms. This thought blocks all 'enterprises', this 'pale cast of thought' makes one 'lose the name of action' itself (3.1); it tells us that no action can be resolutive, that no one might find 'clear' foundation, that no reason and no aim can justify it. That everything, even death itself can be doubted, as an appearance or even a deceit, an illusion.

Having affirmed the doubt, *revocare gradus*[19] becomes impossible. Acting cannot free itself. Hamlet is the decisive figure who casts doubt on the possibility that doing means giving complete form, bringing to an end, arranging, *deciding*. Doubt goes to the ultimate limit: it throws its 'pale pith' over dying itself. Being, or rather doing is incapable of accomplishing itself in death. Death does not *belong* to it, nor, it seems, do the effects of its acting.

Hamlet did not aspire to great undertakings, he had no interest in the crown,[20] nor does his vocation for study in (Lutheran) Wittenberg seem particularly intense (might he and Horatio have discovered traces of Bruno's sojourn there?). If the past had not condemned him to inaction, the problem of the meaning of acting as

---

19 '[T]o recall your steps', see Virgil, *Aeneid* 6.126–129. [Trans.]

20 And yet, as we shall see, he is able to connive as well or better than his antagonists. But not for his *decisive* cause! And Claudius fears his popularity. Only because he is the son of the 'great' Hamlet? Or should we suspect that it is also because of his ability as an actor, an essential attribute of a 'good' demagogue?

ordering-arranging-accomplishing would never have posed itself. Neither would that of a death that is truly de-cision from the tumult of life. Others 'decide' on the basis of inherited orders which, not being produced by them, cannot *in truth* be known to them. Hence, theirs is never a true decision. Hamlet understands this. He could not deceive himself on this matter. Even death happens to them. Hamlet seems to seek it out but, unable to call his action his own, does not make death *his own*. Revenge itself takes place due to the chain of events of which he is 'innocent' because of the law that dominates historical existence, as if it were its gravitational law: the heterogenesis of ends. Hamlet would like to escape it but to live hidden 'in a nutshell'.[21] (To become 'thin' like Kafka? But upon him *weighs* the necessity of representing and acting . . . 'He's fat . . .' his mother reveals). He is not allowed to forget that to live without doing is denied him. And doing means being-together, in an inextricable *polemos* with all the parts of the drama. How then to 'accomplish oneself'? How can one affirm something as *one's own* in the prison-web of facts? It is this *search* that the dying Hamlet asks should be remembered 'in this harsh world' (5.2). He seeks not the fame of heroes; with respect to this goddess, Fame, he is as *disenchanted* as the fools of the Elizabethan scene, or of Alberti's Momus,[22] who stands as their authentic 'prologue'. Hamlet invites Horatio to continue to live 'to tell my story', so that the motives that necessitated

---

21 Does Hamlet desire the 'bad infinity' of an eternal mourning? The figure of the 'great Father' would exonerate him from acting. Instead, it is precisely what awakens in him the sense of guilt for the *inactuositas* of his own existence—a guilt to which Hamlet would be incapable of reacting as Kafka did. The entire play could be read as a failed *Letter to his Father*.

22 Momus is the name of the protagonist of the eponymous satirical play by the artist, scientist and great Renaissance humanist, Leon Battista Alberti. See his *Momus* (Sarah Knight trans., Virginia Brown and Sarah Knight eds) (Cambridge, MA: I Tatti Renaissance Library, 2003). [Trans.]

his actions are understood—desperate actions to achieve his end. And so he turns to the philosopher, to the one who interprets and explains, and not to the Muse who is song and enigma.

A new story which requires exegesis to be understood: the more action demands that its word be a commanding one, the more painful the awareness that it is determined and conditioned on all sides by facts whose essence the subject is unable to grasp. The will to *knowledge* expresses nothing other than the struggle against this paradox. It is necessary for me to turn to the fact that 'bears' me to force it to reveal its 'ground' to me; I recognize my freedom has nothing to do with the unconditioned, but I nevertheless believe that a 'perfect' knowledge of my 'prison' could provide foundations for my action. I will bear my cause upon myself, to paraphrase Max Stirner, not because I delude myself into being *causa mei* but because I have come to seize, in the *concept* the chain, the web of facts that have 'borne me' to action.

Only knowledge *justifies*. But how can one understand? How can that *fact* that now forces me to act be known? One would need to participate in it so intimately as to become identified with it. Moreover, how can one assert that one knows the past bearer if we necessarily ignore the destination? The past lives in the present that recalls it, but of the future of this present we have nothing but pallid forewarnings. All it seems possible to say is that here-and-now one must fight so that the reasons for what calls to us and wants us to be responsible appears to us as 'evident'.[23] Nevertheless, we are aware

---

23 'In order to perform revenge with conviction, you must believe in the justice of your own cause. This is what we noted before, and the revenge seeker will not believe in his own cause unless he believes in the guilt of his intended victim. [. . .] If the victim's victim is already a killer and if the revenge seeker reflects a little too much on the circularity of revenge, his faith in vengeance must collapse. This is exactly what we have in Hamlet.' René Girard, *A Theatre of Envy* (Oxford: Oxford University Press, 1990), p. 273.

that such an investigation will be unable to reach any kind of indisputable foundation, nor, consequently, permit any 'secure' forecast. A fork in the road appears, then, to spring up: either an acting that presumes to be a decision, but that in reality chains itself to the order of events and the values that have 'spoken' us to this point (despite the awareness that they have led to the present catastrophe); or to insist in the search for evidence that would bring doubt to an end and allow for a grounded decision. Yet this search reveals itself as interminable, since the knowledge of the facts that determine and condition us sinks into a past unknowable in its essence, and therefore never reducible to a *presence*; a past that is perfectly analogous to the 'eternal future' that manifests itself in every action by concealing itself.

The past commands, but why listen to it if we do not know its name? How do we know that it truly destines our actions, our living-acting, if its name remains obscured? The only possible 'obedience' to its voice becomes that of continuing to interrogate it. Interminable 'question'. At each moment, action measures the distance between itself and its own possible foundation, and so between the form of hesitation and referral that characterizes it on the one hand, and that of authentic decision on the other. The by-now irreducible demand for the subject to achieve full clarity about the meaning of all its thoughts and actions clashes with the awareness of historical existence, making it impossible to satisfy the demand. But if acting does not correspond to an 'imperative' that is in-itself evident, it will continue to appear to be commanded, which is to say, incapable of deciding, of conferring a final form to the 'to do', and so to the 'to be' itself.

When the past erupts in its vivid presence, its appearance is so imperious that it seems impossible not to follow it. Historical existence 'naturally' venerates it. Here we find the Father, incorruptible, safe-guarded from our incompleteness, a Hercules who sustains our fragility. Death seems to have rendered his greatness unalterable. Historical existence is tempted to extol the example he provides, passing its time in the study of or the regret for the *consummatum est*.[24] This would perhaps have been Hamlet's 'decision', taken to justify his inertia, had he not received the fatal visitation. Since Hamlet has no vocation for praxis, nothing is more a betrayal of his character than playing it as hysterical and febrile. His appearance is rather lazy, burdened.[25] Hamlet's 'tempo' remains slow throughout the play. To

---

24 'It is finished' or 'it is completed'. Jesus Christ's final words on the cross in John 19:30. [Trans.]

25 This emphasis on the appearance of Hamlet is a moment of genius in Goethe's interpretation in the *Meister* (moreover, did not Ralph Waldo Emerson write that Shakespeare is the father of German literature and the speculative genius of the nineteenth century is a sort of living Hamlet?). He must doubtless appear young (how could he otherwise be so passionately drawn to his mother—and so passionate the son's 'sermon' against her lasciviousness? And yet, as is well known, a problem opens here, because in the 1604 edition, Hamlet is a 'mature' thirty-year-old, whereas in the Pseudo-Shakespearean version published the year before, he is more realistically in his twenties). He must appear Nordic, blonde, pale but above all a little fat. 'The fencing tires him; the sweat is running from his brow; and the Queen remarks: *He's fat and scant of breath* [. . .] "You are spoiling my imagination," cried Aurelia: "away with your fat Hamlets!".' J. W. Goethe, *Wilhelm Meister's Apprenticeship and Travels*, VOL. 2 (Thomas Carlyle trans.) (London: Chapman and Hall, 1907), p. 23. And yet, Meister insists on his idea. If that's how it is, we might say, of the three one must be true: either Hamlet does not resemble his father, whose virile beauty he celebrates; or his horror before his uncle's face derives from the fact that he recognizes himself in it; or—finally—he resembles neither the one or other, both of whom are 'good' brothers. Only he is 'ugly', and so he is painfully aware that he does not appeal to his mother. A Hamlet 'played' in this way would truly be a tasty morsel for an Alfred Jarry!

begin with, he is presented as the one who is willing to linger over a faithful memory. Then the 'visitation' upsets this possibility but in two distinct moments. In the first, the violence of the apparition seems to prevent a response: heart, collect all your strength; nerves, do not age at one blow, remain firm. '[W]ith wings as swift / As meditation [. . .] / May sweep to my revenge' (1.5). Mourning is transformed into a drama, into *Trauerspiel*. It is impossible to 'act it' in private, as a thing of the heart. But the decisive moment is the second one (even if one senses its timbre from Hamlet's very first words). If the past is venerable, why does it ask? How can it be a foundation if its 'presence' is forced to turn to us, to our wretchedness, to implore that it might be 'continued'? Thus, not even the past can be 'perfect'. What hides behind its armour? *Who* is the time that we call past and that instead *insists* here, within the home, more obsessively present than those who inhabit it?

It is at the sight of the father that Hamlet responds with his monologue.[26] The radical doubt over the 'certainty' of death is born of the bitter experience that the past lives. And its life makes us prisoners. But if the past is as 'imperfect' as our present acting, equally in-secure, what right can impose obedience upon us? The past appears armed, but it wanders in search of satisfaction, like the *personae* most alien to the mask of Hamlet. Immortal for not knowing how to die. The son wanted to make an idol of it. Instead, the idol wanders restlessly, *in-sanus*, like his successors but more so. It would like to command; in truth, it pleads. This reveals a state of the world that was previously unimaginable, a universal state of

---

26 Beware of taking the famous monologue as a lyrical 'interlude'! It is firmly rooted in Hamlet's character and in the *drama* as a whole. See W. H. Auden, 'Hamlet' in *Lectures of Shakespeare* (Princeton, NJ: Princeton University Press, 2019). The reference to this lecture is fundamental to my work and, particularly, to the relationship between 'to do' and 'to act' in Hamlet.

insecuritas that grips all the dimensions of time. Time, eternal in all its dimensions, is a single irresoluteness.

Once again: if the past that we believed founded us is 'undecided', how can we obey it? It is 'right' to follow the one who exhibits the highest grade of power, of *actuositas*, who appears to us to be 'in form'. Only he could legitimately command; he alone would deserve the name of mortal god! Yet what appeared here was not the ghost of a powerful king but rather power in ghostly garb. So much a ghost as to have to appeal to us, the weakest, to still have power-to-act [*potere ancora*]! And the ghost of the King shows he is very aware of our weakness; he fears and denounces it from his very first words: 'And duller (*dull*: slow-witted, deaf) shouldst thou be than the fat (*fat*: precisely as Hamlet appears to his mother) weed / That rots itself in ease on Lethe wharf / Wouldst thou not stir in this' (1.5).[27] The unresolved past is forced to turn to those who appear most incapable of realizing it, to implore them to do so.

To me, father? You specifically need me? This question fills Hamlet's silence during the ghost's tale. His mind thinks: how can it possibly be me who is called to end what that Hercules that is my father left undone? But was he such a hero, then? His mind thinks—and while thinking it 'orders': *return to your place, sword*.[28] Has the death of the father opened a vortex that now upsets everything, or has it instead revealed the rottenness of the world? The appearance of the ghost certainly opens Hamlet's eyes—not on a terrible crime but onto the total decadence of those values that appeared to support it. It will thus be necessary to doubt and interrogate them. Value must indeed *value*; an impotent value ceases to be. The past appeals to Hamlet to demonstrate that the values that 'armed' it can still do so.

---

27 The interjections in brackets are by the author. [Trans.]

28 *Torna al tuo posto, spada* is the Italian translation of Hamlet's 'up, sword' (3.3.88). [Trans.]

But now it is understood that these values are the same as the ones that made the father's world crumble. Hamlet intuits all of this—he senses it even before knowing it. A bitter knowledge: roots are inexorable, but the root has ceased to 'bear'. The values that are still spectrally flaunted only have value in the form of catastrophe. But what other values could be pitted against them? The soul of the world is sick, a 'sick soul' like that of Hamlet's mother. Sick from the beginning, in her very womb. But in the name of what can the world's soul be refounded?

The ghost demands vengeance, that is, it demands that the concatenation of action should not be interrupted, that every action should belong to this chain without anyone being able to de-cide[29] it. This means demanding that death continue to appear, that our existence never complete itself in the *act* of dying. A similar moment of vengeance would have been immediately seized by Fortinbras and Laertes. It would have precipitated their action—but precisely because in them the fleet wings of thought in no way 'fly' to their natural destination, which is interrogation and delay. Thought does not race to action; in truth, thought moves nothing. Its interior daemon is pale, not just its appearance. Its wings resemble those of Melancholy, more than those of 'heroic frenzy'.[30] Thought seeks the reasons for acting and this search comports delay and doubt,

---

29 Cacciari writes, *de-cidere*, 'to decide', with the hyphen to emphasize the etymology of the term 'decide': from the Latin *de*, 'off', and *caedere*, 'to cut'. The point being that for the vengeful ghost, the world is a chain of events that includes all actions, without thinking of actions as 'decisive', i.e. as cutting into, or breaking the chain. Thus, actions are subject to the fateful chain of events from which they cannot escape. [Trans.]

30 *Eroici furori*—an allusion to Giordano Bruno's philosophical dialogue *De gli eroici furori* (published in London in 1585, translated into English as *The Heroic Frenzies*), which links infinite love to knowledge of an infinite universe. [Trans.]

producing a suffocating anxiety rather than resoluteness and decision. When the call of thought is dominant, we find ourselves in the situation that Kafka describes in innumerable 'parables': that of the individual blocked before an open door, who meditates upon the 'marvellous' concomitance of the infinity of events that must take place before he can cross the threshold.

But it must be crossed. Despite thought. The step we take will nevertheless be branded with fire. We know that he who is called does not want to 'redeem' the world but is an integral element of its rottenness. We know even more that his values are not even valuable for holding the world in a 'form'. We know, finally, that we cannot abandon the undertaking that the past demands, since, where no decisive act is possible, there survival is of necessity in command, a survival which is not concluded by death but by 'croaking it'.

This world is rejected by Hamlet in its entirety, and yet it remains tragically his. Its vortex grinds him down as it does all its other parts. Where there are no hypocrites, no corrupted, no assassins, there is their 'promise'; for them, the womb is always fertile. Hamlet does not feign any madness when he treats Ophelia as a 'potential' mother. It is the meditation on the meaning of the 'visit' of the father (which had certainly been prepared by that on the mother's wedding— although this latter event would only have led to an inert withdrawal) which convinces Hamlet it is not a case of mere crimes, but of a single *earthquake*. That which wore the mask of power heralded catastrophe. What constituted our root was uprooting violence. And all the *personae* that appear strong and suited to acting, in truth, decide nothing, their 'decision' amounting to nothing but the perpetuation of general corruption. With his 'delirium' Hamlet intends to represent the *de-lirium*[31] of the world. But it is, at once, also the sign of his

31 'Raving' would be more correct, since it is used here as a verb, but this would not allow for Cacciari's play with the Italian for 'delirium', *delirare*, in relation to the question of 'rooting', 'uprooting'. In writing *de-lirare*, he is

lingering meditation. The stronger the impetus with which the ghost wants to compel the will of the son, the more the latter's anguish grows for being unable *in truth* to correspond to the ghost's demand.

The face of the father is that of the night that flees light, not that un-veils and re-veals[32] it. The father is condemned for his crimes; the woes that he bears are the most agonizing. The malignant plant[33] of the father is 'Cut off in the blossoms of my sin', weighed down under the weight of his iniquities, 'with all my imperfections on my head' (1.5). An imperfect dead man because he lived his whole life *lacking*. It is all too easy to intuit that his 'imperfections' are essentially the same as those of the Queen and Claudius. What really fills Hamlet with terror is thus that the voice of the father's spirit is an infernal one.[34] This voice now wants to command him to act. How can he

---

emphasizing *de*, off, away, and *lirare*, the infinitive form of a Latin conjugation meaning 'to plough a furrow.' With the hyphenation, *de-lirare*, Cacciari brings out the idea of delirium as a being off course, breaking away from a ploughed furrow. [Trans.]

32 The Italian *rivela* means to reveal, but Cacciari is again playing with the etymology that he emphasizes via hyphenation. The infinitive *rivelare* is made up of *velare*, or 'to veil' and 're-' to 'go back before' the veiling as well as to repeat again the veiling. So *ri-velare* involves an unveiling that veils anew. The reader should keep this dual sense in mind when Cacciari speaks of 'revelation' as well. [Trans.]

33 In Canto 20 of his *Purgatorio*, Dante puts in the mouth of the King of France Hugh Capet the line *Io fui radice della mala pianta / che la terra cristiana tutta aduggia* (Henry Wadsworth Longfellow translated this as 'I was the root of that malignant plant / Which overshadows all the Christian world). *Malapianta* has since come to signify corrupt origins. [Trans.]

34 It is impossible to conceive a different 'placement' for the ghost. It did not have time to end up in Purgatory. The idea of this 'station', moreover, rings entirely alien to the cultural and theological *milieu* of the Elizabethan epoch. Hence, in this case as well, it is a case of the representation of highly

believe it? How can he harbour the total faith in it that it demands? 'And thy command all alone shall live [within me]'—that may be, but how not to *think it*? It will live in me, yes, but necessarily 'Within the book and volume of my brain' (1.5), in thought, which is precisely the *volumen*, a coiling, a labyrinth of intents and doubts, of attempts and forebodings. By its very nature, the brain re-turns [*ri-volge*] into itself and is unable to find the path of decision if it is not seized by a stronger force that wants decision—'and farther question not'.[35]

Hamlet invokes such a force. But desperately. He hunts for images and pretexts that might impel him to his undertaking. He incites himself to commit it. He wants to believe in it at all costs—but in no sense can he have *faith* in it. Too strong and *slow* are the wings of thought. After the performance [*rappresentazione*], he could 'drink hot blood / And do such business as the day / Would quake to look on' (3.2); but it is only a case of representation; or rather, it is a case of the prologue of the *drama* that he is unable to live through. This is not a case of tracking down proof of his father's murder. Hamlet is certain of it. 'O my prophetic soul' he exclaims at the ghost's words; hence he already had a presentiment of it—however much he perhaps sought to drown his presentiments in the waters of Lethe. His is delay and the seeking of delay. 'What we refer to as way is delay', Kafka will declare.[36] The doubt does not concern Claudius'

problematic, indecisive characteristics in opposition to those classically drawn by Ben Johnson. George Steiner has insisted on this difference in his numerous Shakespearean contributions.

35 An expression repeatedly used in Dante's *Inferno*, for the first time in the third canto, in the mouth of Virgil addressing Charon: *Vuolsi così colà dove si puote / ciò che si vuole, e più non dimandare* (5.95–96) (Longfellow version: 'It is so willed there where is power to do / That which is willed; and farther question not.') [Trans.]

36 Franz Kafka, *The Zürau Aphorisms* (Michael Hoffman trans., Roberto Calasso ed.) (London: Harvill Secker, 2006), p. 26.

guilt; and it is utterly irrelevant whether the Queen is complicit or not[37]—yet she is the sign that it is better to not bring into the world or not to have been born.[38] The doubt does not concern who Hamlet-the-King really is either: 'may be the devil' as the son appears to ask himself, but he knows the answer very well: yes, he is, he's an infernal spirit who cannot bear the light of dawn, condemned to fast (in clear contrast with his lasciviousness) among the flames. Must his 'value' still command? It is no longer possible to forget him; but how can one make oneself 'impregnated' by his cause ('unpregnant of my cause', confesses Hamlet)? The ghost returns to sharpen his 'almost blunted purpose', but the 'tardy son' has not simply dropped his earliest impulse, all *passion* for acting; he has had silently to meditate on the scene of the 'visit', on the whole world that it revealed, on the reasons for the 'dread command' (3.4) that was entrusted to him. And this is why he is 'incapable' now to 'birth' action.[39]

---

37 Girard quite reasonably suspects that Hamlet would like his mother to accomplish the revenge, 'relieving him' of the task. In any case, her evident 'unavailability' to even enter such an order of thinking renders her guilty in the eyes of her son. Any *vis dramatica* would crumble were the Queen to 'ally' with the son! This is one of the reasons that make us seriously doubt that the 1603 version of the play can be attributed to Shakespeare.

38 On this motif of classical tragedy, see Umberto Curi, *Meglio non essere nati* (Turin: Bollati Boringhieri, 2008).

39 It is a strange error of Hegel's to see Hamlet as not doubting '*what* he was to do, but only *how*.' G. W. F. Hegel, *Aesthetics*, VOL. 1 (Oxford: Clarendon Press, 1975), p. 244. It is strange since it completely contradicts what Hegel himself writes on 'romantic' drama in relation to its characters' lack of 'substantial ends' (p. 587). Hamlet's indecision instead concerns precisely the principles or reasons that should support his actions. But not in the way of the classical hero, who stands before distinct and opposed dominions of the divine! Hamlet is suspended between a paternal 'justice', and 'another' that stirs un-formed within him, in pure indeterminacy, without a name.

Yet this does not mean that he is 'idle' ('I must be idle' he says at the start of the performance in the castle, a performance that will reveal nothing he did not already know, but where the 'action' is meant to be powerful enough to force him into vengeance). Does being 'idle' here mean indolence, inactivity? Or does it only show him feigning indifference before the eyes of the King and the gathered court? More than this, the term is a tell-tale sign of Hamlet's character: he must be, he can only be *slow*. The torture of the Cogito, of which Alain Badiou speaks in relation to Beckett, finds its prototype in Hamlet.

Tarrying is itself tiring, disquiet is never at rest in itself. Hamlet acts, but his acting is the mirror of the world's *insecuritas*, the pain[40] of which he discovers in his own roots. To want to restore the world by obeying the command of he whose sins all 'flowered'! Impossible. To recompose the pieces of the world would require *thinking* of another beginning, presupposing a *tabula rasa*. It would be necessary to consider everything that does not appear evident to thought, in its rigorous autonomy, as false. But such a decision is impossible for historical existence. It is impossible for Hamlet. For him, the past, any past, is immanent presence. He is not permitted to cross the Lethe, to forget his father. Neither can he believe that he can reorder the world in accordance with his father. He seeks to act as if he believed it, but his actions—which are compelled to feign belief in a command that he knows comes from hell—cannot proceed if not by attempts, by unreliable pathways; they can only err through improvised gestures and across labyrinths of fate. He is never ready for decisive action—but this is because he recognizes with ever-greater clarity that we essentially 'lack' it. When everything appears to favour

---

40 Cacciari writes *male*, which can be translated as 'pain', 'harm'. or even 'evil'. [Trans.]

it, that is when the brain 'acts' like never before. And it brings every-thing to a halt. He could strike Claudius with laughable ease, but a 'theological' reflection stays his hand: hold back, sword, wait to strike him until you are *certain* that he too is lost. One must assess well: 'that would be scanned' (3.3); one must act only when the reasons for your actions are evident to thought. But for historical existence this means postponement and temporizing.

Hamlet acts, but his actions cannot proceed according to that command that he has received—nor in contradiction to it. In order to oppose it, he would need to be certain of new values, other than those that put the world 'out of joint'. For his 'no' to be legitimate, it must not suffer from any of his father's 'imperfections'. The pallid philosophy he learnt with Horatio, even if it has value has no power, neither on earth nor in heaven. Hence his actions oscillate 'indecisively': Machiavellian, like those of a king when he rids himself of the 'friends' Rosencrantz and Guildenstern; powerful, like those of an 'outlaw' sovereign in the terrible scene of Polonius' murder; ensnared by his own stratagems in the final scene of his feigned madness and the performance at court; right upto the final, increasingly weary 'gestures', almost nostalgic for an end of any kind. There are words of Cioran's that express the situation better than any commentary: 'any gesture performed is not worth defending [. . .] failure [. . .] reveals us to ourselves.'[41]

Hamlet kills Polonius with the same impunity his father would have had. Here he truly shows how the world he detests continues to be his own. Indeed, in the 'prison' there is no space for compassion or repentance: 'Thou wretched, rash, intruding fool [. . .] Take thy

41 E. M. Cioran, *The Trouble with Being Born* (Richard Howard trans.) (New York: Arcade Publishing, 1976), pp. 3 and 17.

fortune'; 'I'll lug the guts into the neighbour room' (3.4). Hamlet is capable of these 'acts' and these words. He possesses the 'will, and strength, and means' (4.4), but his will, strength and means are incapable of ordering a decisive plan of action, of bringing the work to an end. If in the end he executes his father's will, he in no way 'accomplishes it'. He is 'compelled' to exact revenge due to the plans of others, overwhelmed by events, hastening towards a death he has not procured himself. The end corresponds only extrinsically to the content of the will, since such a content cannot convince thought. The 'volume' of thought, as soon as it is agitated, departs from the blood. 'My thoughts be bloody,' says Hamlet in self-exhortation. But it is precisely this 'accord' that is now impossible. Bloody action takes place despite thought; and thought unfolds [*si svolge*] and re-enfolds [*ri-avvolge*][42] without being able to decide.[43]

As soon as his thought runs up against what needs to be done, 'this thing's to do' (4.4), the truly serious 'affair' he is duty-bound to accomplish, Hamlet finds himself a stranger to all surrounding 'orders', that of the courtier as well as that of the Machiavellian politician, as much as the order of philosophy and of honour (at the

---

42 As with earlier instances of *ri-volgere* ('turning towards', 'turning back inwards'), Cacciari is lending conceptual weight to etymology, here suggesting we think together *svolgere* (to 'develop', to 'unfold') and *riavvolgere* (to 'envelop', to 'wind' and 'unwind'—as a ball of wool might be unwound or rewound). The *ri* can be reflexive as well as to mark a repetition. [Trans.]

43 Hamlet's final 'prophecy' and his 'vote' for Fortinbras must be read as testimony to Hamlet's 'realism'. It is not a case of a transfer of power, but of an *abdication*, even a *betrayal*: for is not Fortinbras his father's enemy? Nevertheless, Hamlet recognizes that the realm can only be supported by a 'direct' will-to-power, with vast ambitions, alien to the 'closedness' of castles and family intrigues. The thought of such a will shall know, then, how to *bleed* (and cause to bleed).

same time, the mind is forced to ask itself, with Macbeth, if there is still something serious 'in mortality'; is not everything now 'toys' and 'play'?). And yet he is incapable of 'overcoming them'. He coexists with these orders while thinking of their ruin; he sees all of them with the eyes of the *fool*, in the cemetery.[44] But he too has reached this point. It will not be enough to know or sense the catastrophe to put the world back on track. It will not be enough to understand that no blood can save him for a new Order to manifest itself. Ophelia had described him as the mirror of all virtues—but more correctly he represents the mourning for their loss: mourning for the virtue of the soldier disarmed by ambition, for that of the Machiavellian emptied of will-to-power, for the man of honour no longer deceived, who sees his 'passion' reduced to the abjectness of the mere courtier. But also, for the virtue of the man of thought who, coming face-to-face with the disjointedness of the world, discovers the pallor of thought, the powerlessness to 'move'. Of none of these losses is Hamlet innocent. He is the opposite of the victim as 'beautiful soul'; he intervenes, acts, kills, but 'sporadically'. The impossibility of finding a foundation for his 'purpose' leads not to inaction but to the inability of *cutting* the continuity of time, of 'accomplishing' an epoch and beginning a new one. In this sense, no one in the play decides and so no one can 'save'.[45] Much less can Hamlet do so, as he executes his revenge, which is itself the symbol of the chains of guilt and punishment that

---

44 'Shakespeare is the most poignant reading I know: how much suffering does it take for someone to need to play the clown!' Friedrich Nietzsche, *Ecce Homo* in *The Anti-Christ, Ecce Home, Twilight of the Idols: And Other Writings* (Judith Norman trans., Aaron Ridley and Judith Norman eds) (Cambridge: Cambridge University Press, 2005), p. 91. An identical comment could be placed as an epigraph to works such as *Waiting for Godot* or *Endgame*.

45 An individual can never save an epoch but only express its loss. Take Kierkegaard—is he thinking of Hamlet?

imprison us.[46] But how can these chains be broken? How can we not obey the 'spirit of gravity' of a past that wishes to survive if we are *desperate*? Historical existence knows that the past speaks to us regardless, and yet it acts to 'liberate itself from it', to assert values that 'subvert' those inherited. In the Wittenberg where he wished to retire, perhaps to avoid the 'ghostly visitation', Hamlet could not but have reflected on the fact that the German word *Wert* has the same Latin root as *vertere*![47] But what *Wert* does he have available to him that would justify his will to 'surpass' the already-done and already-said? And even if he had it available in thought, he doesn't in any way show the firm belief of making it count [*valere*]. In this situation, he is forced to follow the *given* Order by manifesting, at once, all its horrendous 'imperfections'. The burning lens of all hypocrisy, as of all illusion; the ruthless critique of every idea of 'completion', as of every flight from the condemnation to act.

The bitterest disenchantment concerning the 'law' he is compelled to follow is manifested in Hamlet's *theatricality*. Having to obey this law is the essential factor of universal 'disharmony'. Hamlet allows us to sense that contrast and the nature of his character in the most

---

46 This is the fundamental problem not only of Girard's work on Shakespeare but also of his entire oeuvre. And yet it already dominated Pavel Florensky's essay on Hamlet from 1905. The tragedy of the work consists, for Florensky, in the representation of the conflict between two incompatible forms of conscience, between two *justices*. *Hamlet*, then, is an example of a true *theomachy*, from this point of view entirely analogous to classical tragedy. But in *Hamlet*, any 'catharsis' is impossible. There is no *deus ex machina* to 'ferry' us to a new religious consciousness.

47 The Latinate root *vertēre* means 'to turn', 'to change', 'to alter' and is related here to historical order as well as to the value (*Wert*) that Cacciari tells us always wills to be—but here in a context where it cannot *de-cide*, cannot cut the continuity of the chain of historical events. [Trans.]

anguished form through his immoderate glorification of his father, in the 'sermon' to his lustful mother, and in the 'contest' with Laertes over who suffers most over Ophelia's grave. No one better than Auden has understood how for Hamlet to do is in truth 'to act'; he is the director-author of the court spectacle and an actor in his own life. Hamlet is 'unfit' to act except by performing; he acts, as we have seen, but always as a 'play at possibilities';[48] he assumes different roles in different situations into which he 'falls' and he plays them out in relation to the different possibilities open to him. And he always finds his own acting inadequate. He may be able to convince others but never himself, because for him 'to act' must ultimately issue in a 'to do'; which is to say, inspire an irresistible passion for the *act*. Instead, it makes him more distant and does so necessarily because the representation or performance is founded on the unbridgeable distance between the representor and represented. It is fiction in essence. What I perform cannot be both what I am and what I do. However hard he tries, Hamlet cannot identify with his roles to the point of making them into his very own life. He performs vengeance because he is unable to accomplish it. He performs and *hence* he is not what he performs. The more he seeks to be his character the more he demonstrates the distance that separates him not so much from what he desires, but from knowing what he desires. The 'to act' is 'perfect' the more it shows itself to be 'autonomous' from the reality of the 'to do'. But if I am missing the 'to do', if it is always missing its end, if it never manages to be *at the end*, it will then always appear in some way as a 'to act'. Therefore, Hamlet does not just happen to be an actor; he is one essentially. Unable to completely impersonate his daemon, to 'satisfy' his own destiny, living instead in the unbridgeable distance between the content of his will and the sense of his action, Hamlet can only 'represent himself'. But

---

48 Auden, *Lectures on* Shakespeare, p. 164.

since this in no way represents his aim, he is therefore 'undecided' as an actor as well. As far away from an 'accomplished life' as from the 'autonomy' of the scene, where thoughts can appear 'bloody' precisely because they cause no blood to run.

Only one part, only one possibility is Hamlet incapable of performing a priori: that of the King. It is a part that is already 'taken', forever. More precisely, it is inexorably 'past', become 'nothing' (4.2) in his eyes. And yet he is the son of that part that has crumbled; it belongs still to his 'body'. 'Not to be . . .': to be the son of No-thing.[49]

The tragedy of historical existence: it can only will itself to be the *protagonist*, but to be the protagonist in the dimension of the 'to do' means being able to decide upon new orders, since, on the one hand, it involves the impossibility of such a decision because of the inexorable recurrence of the already-done, and, on the other, it implies the unfoundedness of the will to surpass it, so all that is left is the *representation of decision*. We encounter here the new form of the tragic. Upon its scene, historical existence interminably performs its own tension towards the accomplished 'to do', which means wandering[50] from shipwreck to shipwreck.

But something unheard of breaks in upon this scene. In the universal performance, the portent of 'another' world appears; in the theatre of 'imperfections', of incompleteness, of feigning, a presence is manifested that does not illuminate the darkness, but that cannot be

---

49 *Ni-ente. Niente* is the Italian word for 'nothing', but the hyphen emphasizes the negation or nothingness of the 'thing' or entity, the *ente*. [Trans.]

50 Cacciari writes *errando*, from the infinitive *errare*, meaning 'to wander', 'to stray', 'to err'. Therefore, to wander is also to 'err', to walk aimlessly, without direction or sense—one might think perhaps of Dante who found himself straying from the righteous path at the start of his *Inferno*. [Trans.]

captured by the darkness. A miracle that undermines all orders of catastrophe, that is victorious over them in defeat itself. Ophelia is the authentic stranger, the truly 'purely mad'. She is the only character who is 'worthy' of her own death. She is put on stage in the encounter with Hamlet spied upon by Claudius and Polonius. But on that stage she does not recite. She lives in silent anguish alongside Hamlet while the others observe the play within a play, spectator-actors all. She lives while she dies, whereas Hamlet performs the will to suicide. She lives in her accomplished silence, while her brother and lover argue over who would be more willing to be buried alongside her.

Ophelia is a stranger to the theatre of the world in the same way as her god: free love, which demands nothing and accomplishes itself in not being understood or loved.[51] The others croak but in *Hamlet* there is one who dies: Ophelia. This means that in the vortex of historical existence a 'mystery' is preserved that surpasses it. Hamlet perhaps intuited it in his first encounter with Ophelia. But only to immediately forget it, immersed as he was in his father's visitation, despairing before the sight of lies and crimes. The truth is that Hamlet is as incapable of love as all other 'actors'. Ophelia's love is a possibility for which that the theatre of the world makes no provision.

The more Hamlet is incomplete and unfinishable, all the 'surer' appears Ophelia's demise, her shipwreck. She has no need to declare her love. To her, offering her love seems the same as feeling it. She has no need to perform it to convince herself of it. The play's most terrible scene is that of the meeting between the 'mad' Hamlet and Ophelia's innocence. Hamlet rejects her gift with unparalleled violence. But why? Had he not written that he loved her (no doubt, in weak verses, sighs with poor 'scansion')? And if he loved her, why

---

51 'Shakespeare draws with a supreme delicacy this image of pure, metaphysical beauty, which contains something of the divine grace of the marionette.' Nadia Fusini, *Donne fatali* (Roma: Bulzoni, 2005), p. 34.

not confide in her? In contrast, he 'horrifically' comes to confuse her with his mother, imagining her as a breeder of sinners if she does not hide away in a monastery. What actor could ably pronounce the words 'I loved Ophelia' (5.1) after having struck her with such insults? But that is what must happen, because even Hamlet's scene, his part, slinks between the skies and the earth. Hamlet is not his father, neither Claudius nor Polonius, nor anyone else, but he is unable to abandon their 'representation'. Only Ophelia, the 'possibility' she personifies, cannot be imprisoned in the general 'play'. She can be used, in the same way as her father uses her, as Hamlet uses her to give vent to his indecision. But she 'obeys' their violence as though turning her other cheek. And in the end, she returns to the Non-place from which she mysteriously came.

Hamlet's words violate her in the most odious ways, but they do not kill her. She does it. She is the only one capable of doing it. Gathered around her tomb, but infinitely far from being able to understand its meaning, everyone else is left merely with the shame of still having 'to act', whereas she, the young girl, the weakest, exhibited the strength to de-*pose* her own spirit. Hamlet's 'guilt' is reflected in Ophelia's *decision*; he can see in her the dis-orderly fashion in which she pursued her 'purpose'.

The tragedy ends with Ophelia's burial. The rest is inevitable survival, vengeance included. The likes of Fortinbras, Claudius and Laertes will continue, in their apparent lives and deaths. Horatio's philosophies will continue. Hamlet himself will continue, since the consciousness of the incompleteness of action must endlessly return, and the story is marked by his delays, by his 'force' that withholds and retards. But how could Ophelia return? Her death is *true* like her love. She will not ask for compensation or revenge. She will not 'reincarnate' in any ghost. Her character is complete. The 'judgement' she has issued on this world is complete in the only form proper to purity: silence.

Neither does she pray for the 'out of joint' world to be saved by that love which her character expresses. Not even with prayer does she break the purity of her silence. Here lies the great difference with the character of Gretchen in *Faust*, which Goethe no doubt imagined while thinking of Ophelia. In the 'Night' scene, Mephistopheles sings a song on his guitar, 'ein moralisch Lied' (a moral song) (v. 3680) in order to capture the young girl. The song sarcastically echoes the 'distract[ed]' Ophelia in her encounter with the Queen (4.5). The devil uses Ophelia's own words to violate her again; he inverts her delirium of regret for all the St Valentines days she would never enjoy into a vulgar means of seduction. In this way, Mephistopheles 'foresees' for Gretchen the same destiny as for Ophelia. But Gretchen is *assumed* in the mystical Chorus and sits alongside the glorious Mater who is capable of purifying what she has loved. This symbol is denied to the harsh law of tragedy. It is extraordinary how Shakespeare wishes to insist on the fact that Ophelia will be granted no sacred terrain. '[F]or charitable prayers, / Shards, flints and pebbles should be thrown on her,' says the priest with Christian compassion. 'Must there no more be done?' (5.1); no, nothing more, not even singing a requiem for her. Ophelia knows no 'beyond' of her misery. Nor does her death redeem her murderers, who, having buried her, must continue with their 'imperfect' designs, prisoners of one another.

Gretchen's final words are those that 'bear her up there', whereas Ophelia's are so desperate that they are 'cited' by Mephistopheles in his little seducer's song. Ophelia remains fixed as the sign of contradiction. The world does not recognize her, nor does she know how to reconcile with it. Could she ever, instead of the song, pray for mercy and repentance? This would be to allude to a hope that nothing in the play justifies. Only as negative theology is hope possible in the world of *Hamlet*. Any other word would have transformed her from perfect symbol of a 'realm' that is not of this world into sentimental yearning, a quietist appeal to universal reconciliation. But she must fall in order to show the incommensurable wretchedness of the world in comparison to her measure of love.

Nobody repents for their part in the theatre of the world, however much they can see its horror. 'O, my offence is rank it smells to heaven [. . .] Pray can I not [. . .] But, O, what for of prayer / Can serve my turn?' (3.3). How can the murder be forgiven when the assassin holds onto the fruit of the crime? Nobody prays, nobody repents, nobody forgives. Everyone is chained to their side, the side they have taken, despite seeing its fault. Everyone, but not Ophelia, because she does not take a side. The immense difference between Hamlet and the others is that he is aware of the impotence of revenge, but he would not know what to oppose to it other than retreat, renunciation, flight—were he not to grasp, in the end, its impossibility. Forgiveness too is a verb he ignores. Ophelia does not delude us into thinking that this supreme *action* is possible for those who crawl across the scene of the world, but precisely by not deluding us she permits us to grasp its idea. Aside from the revelation that the 'body of the King' is 'nothing', that it is this 'nothing' that still dictates norms to us and compels us to the chain of action whose origin and end we ignore (other than to acknowledge that we must participate in the 'play of possibilities'), there is that 'melodious lay' (4.7) of Ophelia's pure folly that accuses nothing and prays for nothing, a pure 'lament' of love. Perhaps it is to hide the shame of being unable to obey this lament that Laertes and Hamlet cry out to be buried with the young girl. Hamlet, who has betrayed her more than anyone, will feel the shame more than anyone, almost to the brink of repentance. But just as no Mephistopheles has accompanied him in his tale, so too no Gretchen will call for his salvation.

TWO

Castles

The Castle's K. has become a *mythos* just as indispensable as that of Hamlet. The 'castle' is a symbol, and like all symbols, it is inexhaustible; the tale of K.'s 'struggle' *against* it has the standing of a myth.

In *Hamlet*, the subject is powerless to constitute himself as the *substratum* of decision and, while he signals the possibility of new 'orders' without ever being able to name them, he is compelled to obey the logic of *facts*. This is an aporia the prisoner runs into, a condition that does not prevent him from willing and acting, but that marks each of his actions with their incompleteness.

The *facts* weigh upon K. with equal force, but their mass has coagulated as though in an impenetrable geological stratum. Hamlet has a genealogy; he belongs to a history that is shared with other parts of the play. K., on the other hand, is a stranger, '*ein Fremder*'. This is so, first, because K. is 'abstracted' from any bloodline or location, catapulted *ex nihilo* into a situation destined to condition him in every way; but second, he is a stranger because this situation appears to us a mere *datum*, not the product of a 'project', no matter how 'mineralized'. Thus, acting manifests itself as so much a prisoner of the order of facts as to render inconceivable the very timbre of decision. Every gesture, every word that, knowingly or not, exceeds its necessary rhythm is considered an inexplicable *phenomenon*, something that the 'laws of nature' which the 'community' obeys do not foresee and cannot interpret. An event that, nevertheless, is given, undeniably, a 'monstrous' *case* that it would be impossible to pretend to ignore. A *single* case, at least for now, which constitutes an imperceptible, feeble alarm bell, perhaps merely imagined but which in any case one must consider. The dominant 'paradigm' is called upon to demonstrate its impotence—certainly not through unpleasant and, ultimately, dangerous contrasts, but by exhibiting the *fact* of absolute isolation, irrelevance, ineffectuality. The fact of the impossibility of *deciding*.

It was not *yet* like that for Hamlet. Yes, he is a *solitary* individual, as far as the thought that corrodes action is concerned, but the idea of revenge constitutes a common horizon. Hamlet is 'expert' in the language of the 'prison', and so understands the horror and the crisis. Precisely what is 'common' is precluded to K. This is not because it alludes to some esoteric, secret dimension. On the contrary, the 'autochthonous' stubbornly try to convince K. that their language is perfectly 'natural', self-evident, and that all 'cases' must be reduced to it unless they want to result in folly. The dynamic of the two figures thus appears opposed and complementary: Hamlet sets out from the order of facts so as, vainly, to undermine sovereignty; from the beginning K. appears as a stranger, 'ontologically' so, and seeks to understand and participate in a 'system' that appears to him impenetrable. Both express a will to knowledge. Hamlet must know 'his own' past so as to found his action. K. is now pure ek-sistence,[1] 'uprooted', and yet he yearns to know and rationally ground his own being-thrown.

---

1 Cacciari is alluding to the Heideggerian term for existence, which the German philosopher sometimes renders as *Ek-sistenz* to emphasize the way *Dasein* 'stands out' in the world, and from the world of entities, as the only being for whom its existence is at issue. See Martin Heidegger, *Being and Time* (John Macquarrie & Edward Robinson trans) (Oxford: Basil Blackwell, 1962), '§9 The Theme of the Analytic of *Dasein*'. [Trans.]

He wants his 'case' to be explained in light of a norm, so that it ceases to be a mere 'case'. But the norm, in order to recognize him, would have to essentially mutate. And K. cannot ask for this and indeed never does. How could an *individual* refound a *common* language? Hamlet fights to 'free himself of it' at the same time that he is compelled to obey his father's command. Instead, K. seems to struggle fully to enter the web of *facts* into which he says he has been summoned, but he demands that it reveal his own foundation, the reason for his existence. He wants its *name*—a name that would ring comprehensible, evident to him. A name cut to his own 'measure'. From here begins the interminable game of interpretations. Hamlet knows the laws of the 'prison' in their very groundlessness and experiences their foundering. K. wants those laws to recognize and 'satisfy' him, he wants to 'inhabit' them—an inadmissible desire, because it would result in their 'catastrophe'. The law, they tell K., is not something that has a foundation, *it is the foundation*; the law is not legitimate because a Value founds it, it itself justifies every form of acting. Every power constitutes itself in the ambit of the law's Power, showing [*mostra*] itself without needing to 'demonstrate itself' [*dimostrarsi*]. Outside of the law's ambit, acting is non-power, the nothing of power—and since 'to be' can be translated as 'to do', it is *nothing* at all.

The earth which in *Hamlet* opened up under the sovereign's feet, swallowing up the prince himself, in *Das Schloss* (*The Castle*) has as if closed up again after the catastrophe. It is a mass that no longer requires 'joints' and appears to have absorbed every contradiction. Conflict inhabits the inside of Hamlet's palace; the term itself is incomprehensible in *The Castle*. If a trace of it appears, it is, so to speak, imported. 'It comes' with K., or it ends up being a very remote memory of a painful secret, as in the case of Amalia. Hamlet is the *home's* stranger; K. seeks to become part of it, unable to accept that the crisis or vortex signalled by the figure of Hamlet is irrevocably *closed*.

Das Schloss: that which is closed, which cannot open (*ent-schliessen*), which can endure precisely because it does not allow itself to be opened. But the Schloss, the Closed,[2] is not so because it encloses a secret that can or must be defended. Were that so, it would immediately evoke the idea of its opening. A secret is what allows 'discovery'. K. thinks as follows: language, norms, the life that I observe *must* have a key that allows me to comprehend them, to interpret them 'rightly'. And the 'answer' is always the same: your question fails because there is nothing to discover, no arcanum to unveil. It is 'evident' that the law of facts is *closed* in on itself, and that this life is founded in its entirety upon it. The law of facts refers only to itself; it is an irrefutable tautology.

Nevertheless, the castle evokes very different ideas; as a translation of Das Schloss, it rings extremely unfaithfully.[3] The castle is 'that' which opens up to the pilgrim, which has truly opened itself to the King who lives there. The 'palace of wisdom' displays two faces in the *Zohar*: it safeguards the Concealed [*Occulto*] beyond all concealment, but it is at once the place in which the Concealed kisses the lover who sought the Light within it. The castle can be 'seven times encompassed with lofty walls', but he who is truly directed towards his own End will know how to cross the seven doors and the seven moats 'as firm ground'.[4] The symbol of the castle recurs in

---

2 The noun *Schloss* can mean 'castle' or 'lock'. As a verb, *schliessen*, it means 'to close'. [Trans.]

3 On the symbol of the castle and its possible relationship to Kafka's novel I have drawn on numerous suggestions in the study by Antonio M. Sicari, *Nel 'castello interiore' di santa Teresa d'Avila* (Milan: Jaca Book, 2006), (especially the introduction 'L'inaccessibile castello: Da Franz Kafka a santa Teresa'), although I develop my argument from a different perspective than the author's religious-apologetic one.

4 Dante, *Inferno*, Canto 4, lines 107–9. [Trans.]

all mystical traditions, and always in this sense: it grants access to its inner chamber to all those who proceed along the 'right path'.[5]

The voyage is an essential part of the castle itself; the rooms or stations through which one reaches its heart are integral parts of it. It is inconceivable to inhabit the castle without crossing all the *moradas* that leads to its interior.[6] Ultimately, this is but the final *morada*. The final dwelling is nothing but the path to its *eschaton*, the point that expresses all its energy as inseparable from the labour and risk of the journey. The *moradas* do not represent stopping points, moments of rest or forgetting, but the culminating aspects of the struggle of the soul for exodus, to come out of itself and reveal its own ek-static[7] nature.

The 'composition' of the castle corresponds to the *impetus* of soul 'injured by love', at the moment of the *vuelo del espíritu* (soul's flight) (Teresa of Avila) that rises up there like a flame. Over seven days, through seven 'enclosures' (Ruysbroeck's *sept clôtures*),[8] seven rooms and seven skies, whether or not in the end a perfect *unio mystica* comes about, the castle—however composite and complex

----

5 The quotation is from the opening verse of Dante's *Inferno*. The *diritta via* is literally the 'straight path', but it carries with it the sense of 'righteous path'. [Trans.]

6 The reference is to St Teresa of Avila's *El Castillo Interior* or *Las Moradas* (*The Interior Castle*, or *The Mansions*), describing a spiritual journey through the seven rooms, mansions, of the soul depicted as a castle. Passage through these rooms would ultimately lead to spiritual unity with God. [Trans.]

7 The notion of the *Ekstase*, of the ek-static, is drawn from Heidegger, and plays on the etymological Greek root-meaning of the term as 'standing outside.' See Heidegger, *Being and Time*, p. 377 and n. 2. [Trans.]

8 John van Ruysbroeck (Jan van Ruusbroec) (1293/4–1381), Augustinian canon and Flemish mystic, author of *The Seven Enclosures* (*c.*1346–50). [Trans.]

it appears—remains the place that hosts, the symbol of the edifice of the soul that safeguards, in its most impenetrable penetration, the soul of the King. The opposite of the Schloss.

And yet the castle opens only to he who has *decided* to confront the *moradas*—with an unwavering will, a will that appears as the very essence of being-there [*esserci*].[9] A superhuman will is necessary to penetrate the castle, one capable of realizing the accord between the fullness of Marta's doing and of Maria's contemplation; one that is capable of winning [*vincere*], or rather, of *triumphing-over* [*super-vincere*] the 'great war' with the powers that make us 'depend' upon worldly *bona-impedimenta*, '*sin otra luz y guía / sino la que en el corazón ardía*'[10] (Juan de la Cruz). Those who do not *de-cide* and separate themselves from any will to possess 'down here',[11] and do not decide to *transcend themselves* to the point of listening within themselves to the *divinum silentium*, will fatally lose themselves along the way, however virtuous or wise they might be.

Hence the castle is 'transitable' only to the extent that it is recognized as the image of our most intimate spiritual struggle. But

---

9 *Esserci* means 'being there' in the everyday sense of 'I'll be there'. It also happens to be the Italian translation for Heidegger's *Dasein*, which though in ordinary German often simply means 'exist', also breaks down into 'being there'. This seeks to capture the fundamental trait of that being who is 'thrown' into the world, which—as Heidegger puts it—we ourselves are. Heidegger uses *Dasein* to escape the metaphysical, sociological, anthropological, etc., assumptions contained in the notion of the 'human subject'. [Trans.]

10 'Without light or guide, / save that which burned my heart' ('On a Dark Night' by St John of the Cross). [Trans.]

11 This is a curious grammatical construction, until we remember the root of the term 'decide' in 'to cut'. Hence, the meaning is that those who do not choose to cut themselves off from, to separate themselves from the 'will to possess', will be led astray. [Trans.]

all around it spread 'imperfect paths' (Juan de la Cruz). The path marked by the *moradas* runs straight but is arduous and rugged. There are many more comfortable paths that flank it. They too ascend but, ultimately, lead nowhere; these paths entrust themselves to our faith in the possession of our freedom and knowledge, 'sure' only of these virtues. Yet these paths are also part of the castle, precisely because one is not allowed to enter it without confronting *all* of life's dangers. Once one passes through imperfect paths, the castle immediately becomes a Schloss. Its centre is 'conquerable' only if the old man dominated by the will to conquest *dies*, and upon his face falls the *noche oscura*, the dark night.

The castle is not, then, a fortress; it is not a fortified acropolis, rigidly defined in its high bastions. The castle *are* roads, paths, rooms, in each of which take place distinct spiritual struggles. The castle is its *çerco* [ring], its *arrabal* [surrounds], its *moradas*, its *piezas* [parts] and, finally, the *cámara* [chamber] or veritable *palacio del Rey* [King's palace]. The castle *are* also the various dangers posed by the roads that seduce and the encounters with dia-bolic powers that can always occur along them. Losing the path that leads to the *puerta de entrada* [front entrance] is a possibility immanent to the castle's composition. In its labyrinth it *must* always remain open.

The roads of the castle are the opposite of a solitary journey. Along each step of the way, one encounters *amigos* [friends], *parientes* [relatives], functionaries and messengers who live in the *palacio* or in its nearest rooms, but also *vasallos* [servants] who live *en los aposentos bajos*, in the lower lodgings, at the foot of the castle's slope. But one can also bump into *legiones de demonios*, who bar or divert one's path. The 'drama' is that the figure and voice of the demons are no different from those of angels. Together, from the start, they form a 'family'; everyone lives in the castle and is necessary for us to symbolize it.

That is how the castle appears in Teresa of Avila, in Juan de la Cruz, in Carmelite mysticism, all of which appear to recapitulate, via myriad secret and manifest channels, Andalusian Islamic traditions, cabalistic traditions, as well as Flemish and Rhenish ones. It is a voyage *within* the castle of the soul that, to succeed, must pass through the levels and stations (*maqam* in Ibn 'Arabi, *moradas* in Teresa) of perfect obedience, of abandonment, of pure 'poverty', of the freedom from all ties to everything that is *not* God (that independence from the worlds of which the Quran speaks, III, 92), until the Goal [*Mèta*][12] is reached, which will represent the negation of all possession, the *non-station*, the inconceivable and ineffable proximity, the paradoxical conjunction of unity and distance. In the same way that the 'palaces' of the *Zohar* 'open', so do the *castillos* of Sufism and of the Carmelites. Their doors are not merits, they are not virtues, strength or knowledge that we possess. The Lord of the castle '*es muy amigo de humildad*' [is a real friend of humility], our 'calculations' will never be able to conquer him.[13] Our oration, which coincides with our abandonment, our *impetus* of love, our *voracity* of love—as María Zambrano said with reference to Juan de la Cruz—might be able to. But precisely such *voracity* is 'beyond good and evil', expressing a superhuman strength. To realize such abandonment, it is necessary to over-conquer-oneself [*super-vincersi*]; it requires a will-to-power that is superior to all worldly power. Never as here, then, does the will affirm itself as the essence of being-there.

---

12 Cacciari appears to be alluding to the Latin *mēta*—which is very close to modern Italian *meta*—for 'end, 'goal' or 'boundary'. [Trans.]

13 'Humility gives everyone, even the lonely and the desperate, his strongest tie to his fellow men. Immediately and spontaneously, too, albeit only if the humility is complete and lasting' (Kafka, *Zürau Aphorisms*, p. 105). This is an unequivocal example of how Franz K. should not be 'equivocated' with K.!

The castle 'opens' itself because its 'centre' is not something that can be grasped, a final foundation, but rather a non-station, a non-foundation, *Abgrund*. It is 'open' because it symbolizes infinite self-transcendence. If its 'centre' could be captured like a fortified citadel, a *Festung* [fortress], as soon as success is achieved, the castle would cease to exist. Once seized, the Schloss would no longer be a Closure [*Chiuso*],[14] it simply would not be. Those who consider a castle to be a Schloss necessarily seek to destroy it: *Ent-schlossenheit*. They decide to take-away[15] the castle. But taken-away the object of conquest, its meaning too is removed: the hands of the 'conqueror' are left empty, as in the outcomes of certain knightly quests, where the Grail's castle conceals itself in the very instant that it appears nearest and most luminous.

Here is the perhaps insoluble enigma around which we must continue to inquire: is das Schloss in reality a castle to which K. has lost the key, which K. can no longer interpret 'truthfully'? Alternatively,

---

14 *Chiuso* means 'closed' but also 'pen' or 'sheepfold'. It is employed in this sense in Dante, *Purgatorio*, Canto 3. [Trans.]

15 The two-word hyphenated expression *tolto-via* means to 'to take away', from *togliere*, 'to take', and *via*, 'away'. *Togliere* is also frequently used in Italian to translate Hegel's *Aufheben*, an ordinary German word that combines three distinct meanings: 'to cancel', 'to preserve' and 'to raise up'. Hegel, however, speaks only of the former two senses—although it has been argued that the third meaning is also implied. While many English translations use the early-modern word 'sublate' to render the technical term, which had the meaning 'to remove', I have left the more literal term, which has the added benefit of being a direct translation of the Italian (for a discussion of *Aufheben*, see Terry Pinkard's translator's note to G. W. F. Hegel, *The Phenomenology of Spirit* [Terry Pinkard and Michael Baur trans and eds] [Cambridge University Press: Cambridge, 2018] pp. *xl–xli*). It should be noted that Cacciari is not himself a dialectical thinker, indeed he develops a powerful critique of any dialectical process that proceeds through a resolutory pacification of conflicting elements. [Trans.]

is it really a Closure, so that K. does not intend the paradox into which he ends up falling, when he wants to eliminate that which he stubbornly pursues? Or perhaps it *was* a castle, which has completely lost its originary 'figure'? Can what remains of the castle represent the Schloss, or even its forgetting? Furthermore, is the forgetting of the castle rendered possible by the fact that no one is capable of intuiting its form any more, of following its contours, of loving it, because each path, each station is now interpreted merely as a closed door, a *lock* (this is the original meaning of Schloss) to be forced? Or is it the castle itself that is transformed—according to a story that we are not told—into a tangle of hierarchies, commands and figures that no longer guide, no longer destine, which appear to be diabolical imitations of those 'paths' and those rooms, of those angels and those demons of the mystical *castillos*?

It is a beautiful winter morning, contrasting with the night of his arrival, when K. for the first time sees das Schloss 'distinctly outlined in the clear air'.[16] And it appears, rendered clearer still by standing out against the white of the snow, analogous to the *castillos*. It was not an old-style *Ritterburg*, a knight's stronghold, surrounded by towers and moats; nor a *neuer Prunkbau*, a lavish new building, a wealthy city palazzo; nothing like a well-designed and compact construction, but a vast complex of differently sized buildings set close together. We cannot tell whether the tower itself, which would be the high point of a *Ritterburg*, is a part of another habitation or of a church. The nearer K. comes, or thinks he does, the more the Schloss disappoints him. It is '*ein Städtchen*', '*ein recht elendes Städtchen*', a really wretched little town, even less: 'a poor kind of collection of cottages',[17] a hamlet that reminds K. of his hometown ('to this

---

16 Franz Kafka, *The Castle* (Anthea Bell trans.) (New York: Oxford University Press, 2009), p. 10.

so-called Schloss his Heimatstädtchen was very similar'). K. glosses over these revealing observations in the same way that, when he again takes up his walk after the meeting with the schoolteacher, he glosses over the fact that the 'main street of the village'[18] along which he passed did not lead to the Schlossberg, but merely 'went close to it', only to then turn away, 'as if on purpose', without ever leading towards the goal and without ever leaving the village. K. doesn't leave the village; neither does he move away from it, nor does he approach the Schloss; in the end, he 'tore himself away [*riss er sich*]'[19] from the high street to find himself in a narrow lane where the snow is so high as to block his passage.

From his first 'sortie', K. proceeds to sink into immobility. All his going is a circling of the goal to the point of losing the strength to continue. He continually 'tears himself' from the place or house in which he finds himself, only to return exhausted. Does the reason for failure lie within him? Does it lie in the powers that stand against him? And what form does it take? Is it to be found in these powers' 'complicity' with one another, deeper than their apparent enmity? One thing is clear and is in any case essential: that nothing, in substance, differentiates Dorf [village] and Schloss; that the very image of the latter is of a wretched village and that the unbroken path between the two proceeds—insofar as it can be experienced— through its whole length. '"There's no distinction," the schoolmaster said, "between the local people and the castle"'. The same idea comes to K. in the mayor's office: between *Amt und Leben*, life and offices, there is pure coincidence; it is spoken to him by Olga ('Yes, it is said that we all belong to the castle, and there is no distance at all, no gap

---

17 Kafka, *Castle*, p. 11.
18 Kafka, *Castle*, p. 13.
19 Kafka, *Castle*, p. 13.

to be bridged');[20] it is demonstrated to him by the ease with which Barnabas is able to 'pass through' the doors and rooms that K. deems barriers. And Frieda repeats that Klamm is always with them . . .

'*Kein grosser Unterschied*', no separation, quite the contrary: there is no significant difference. The village is never 'interrupted', nor is the 'chain' of figures that are interlinked with the Schloss. It is a *plenum*, all the more suffocating the more each of its elements appears to emerge from the void. From the functionaries that one only glimpses but whose only voice is that of Klamm—when from the en*closure* of his hotel room he calls Frieda—to the liaison officers, who may instead be 'surprised' and forced to speak, the village secretaries, the mayor, Barnabas' messengers, the helpers, the series of demonic-clownish servants who accompany the functionaries— there is no pause, no interruption. Nor is the relationship clear, 'calculable'. Everything holds together, and no one 'dialogues' with anyone else. No barrier and no 'transgression'. The *plenum* is made even more evident by the double-character of each *person*: Sordini- Sortini, Momus-Klamm; the herd of servants could live as true lords in the Schloss. Even the Lord from Alfred Kubin's *The Other Side* was a similar Proteus. And Momus is, of course, a *nomen-omen*:[21] the god of disguise, of the double, who, like the Shakespearian 'fool', is capable of both the irony that dissolves as well as that which opens the eyes and reveals. (What's Momus' game in the episode of the missed interrogation? To mark an effective possibility, to deceive, to force K. to halt his investigation? Or all this, together, like 'together' stand all the functions of the Dorf–Schloss 'system'?).

---

20 Kafka, *Castle*, p. 172.
21 The name is a sign. The saying is thought to originate with Plautus. In Ancient Greece, *Mômos* was the deity personifying satire and mockery, a name etymologically related to *momphé*, 'blame, reproach'. [Trans.]

The compactness, the density of this world. As in a gnostic cosmos, the absence or ineffability of the Beginning [*Principio*] generates a multiplication of intermediate entities. The in-between teems with presences whose nature escapes all precise definition, which can switch names and roles, where angels and demons interweave and are mixed in their very struggle. How could someone who finds themselves 'thrown' in such a world make any distinctions? Even the world of the *castillos* was replete with figures, as we've seen, but all ordered according to *one* light, proceeding from the voice that calls from the ground–non-ground of the soul. It was an *illuminated* density, a *verklärte Nacht*.[22] Whereas the functionaries of the Schloss are fearful of the day, the terms that mark their role are 'sinisterly' similar to those imagined by Teresa: *mayordomos* [butlers], *maestresalas* [headwaiters], *alcaides* [wardens], *amigos* [friends]. But they do not form the *transitus* through the *noche oscura*. Rather, they inhabit it 'steadfastly'; they identify themselves with it. And so K. seems to remain *en el çerco* [the ring] of the *arrabal* [outskirts], in the surroundings, adjacent to the castle. In truth, he is in his *closure*, stranger and prisoner at the same time.

One fact is certain, and it is worth repeating it: in the clear air of the morning, in the light that more sharply outlines its figures, the Schloss appears very similar to a *castillo*, however wretched a state it finds itself in. But it is impossible to distinguish the different paths leading to it, to discriminate the 'straight' path from the imperfect and interrupted routes. There is only one, and it appears to turn upon itself in a vicious circle. It is not 'inaccessible' like the castle path, but almost 'immobile'; a road that sinks into itself and comes to a halt. Is this an ironic-desperate reversal of the station–non-station that

---

22 The implicit reference is to Arnold Schoenberg, op. 4, *Verklärte Nacht* (Transfigured Night) composed in 1899. [Trans.]

concluded the castle itinerary? The castle has 'diabolically' been transformed into a Schloss. Or is it that K.'s mind cannot imagine it in another form? Or do Schloss and K. together represent the two faces of the complete forgetting of the symbol of the castle?

Schloss and castle appear similar, but this likeness cannot be 'worked upon' by K. In his mind, there is place only for the image of the Schloss. For him, it is a case of proceeding towards a power *other* than himself, from which to grasp the sense of his own presence and his own destination. That power does not drive him out—it *leaves him be* in the absolute *indecision* about his role. The demand that moves K. is that this power should decide for him unequivocally. To achieve this aim, he uses every possible intermediary as a mere tool. He hangs on to it as he does to Barnabas' arm in the second attempt to 'touch' the Schloss' doorway. The same love of which he is capable is only that of the *uti*[23]—as such, he is a priori 'condemned' to being unable to 'save'. The castle 'opens' to those who enter into themselves, turning to their own 'ground' with free love as their only impetus. For all other 'intentions', it is the Closed, which cannot be penetrated if not by being destroyed. And how could its intermediaries favour such an end? Hence K.'s tussle between trust and incredulity when it comes to these intermediaries, his spasmodic search for messengers, 'passages' between village and Schloss, each time contradicted by disillusion over their true powers. 'In the light' of the castle, K. is unaware of *everything* that those powers truly 'disclose': inner collectedness, abandonment, patience. A stranger to them, the castle could not but appear to him in the form of the Schloss, and his struggle transforms itself into an interminable interpretation over the way to access it. Like Hamlet, he struggles and acts, but his acting must therefore remain unfinished. Like Hamlet,

23 Latin for 'in order that', 'as', 'when'. [Trans.]

he confides in the force of his intent, but the impatience at achieving its end itself becomes the force that always pushes him away.[24] The sin that expelled us from Paradise is the same one that prevents us from returning to it, in a saying from the Zürau aphorisms.[25]

K. is '*Ein Fremder*'. Above all, to himself. In passing, he recalls having a wife and son; a mere aside, without nostalgia. And of being a land surveyor, but only when he is ordered to immediately leave the Count's land; before which he showed no sign of knowing either where he found himself nor who had summoned him when he suddenly woke: '"What village have I strayed (*verirrt*) to, then?" he asked. "Is there a castle in these parts?"'[26] The night before, immersed in 'mist and darkness',[27] he had left the main road and crossed a bridge to reach the village. He had lingered for some time on the bridge, looking up '*in die scheinbare Leere*', in the apparent emptiness. What was the bridge he was about to cross? When at the end of the first day it is once again completely dark, and he meets Arthur and Jeremiah at the inn, he in no way recognizes his old assistants for whom he had told Schwarzer he was waiting.

'Well, so who are you?' he asked, looking from one to the other. 'Your assistants,' they replied. 'That's right, they're the

---

24 That of the 'impatience at the heart of error'—which is to say, of believing, in error, that the end is 'exhaustible', that 'proximity' can be 'overcome' to the point of 'touching' the goal—constitutes the dominant theme of various of Blanchot's 'exegeses' of Kafka. Error, after all, is inevitable, or avoidable only at the cost of another 'sin', that of carelessness. See Maurice Blanchot, *The Space of Literature* (Ann Smock trans.) (Lincoln, NE: University of Nebraska Press, 1982), p. 78.

25 Kafka, *Zürau Aphorisms*, p. 5.

26 Kafka, *Castle*, p. 5. [translation modified —Trans.]

27 Kafka, *Castle*, p. 5.

assistants,' the landlord quietly confirmed. 'What?' asked K. 'Do you say you're my old assistants who were coming on after me and whom I'm expecting?' They assured him that they were. 'Just as well, then,' said K. after a little while. 'It's a good thing you've come.'[28]

Had they really been 'his' assistants, how can he ask them if they have any idea about land surveying? And immediately accept their answer: 'no'? And if they're not 'his', why allow himself to be immediately convinced of the opposite? Neither they nor he belong to the past of K. He has come here, and here appears to be his beginning. From this beginning he can in no way 'free' himself. '*Auswandern kann ich nicht*'; I cannot yet emigrate. What else might have lured him '*in dieses öde Land*', in that desolate land, if not the irrepressible desire (*Verlangen*) of remaining there? So, something must, *necessarily*, have summoned him there. What?

The castle itinerary unfolds by re-placing ever higher the stations that have been traversed, not by forgetting them. Instead, in K., it's as if what he was and had done was now 'unusable'. Setting out precisely from that single 'property' he appears to have been left with: the job of land surveyor. What tore him away from the past? A nostalgia for leaving? An irrevocable summons? Hamlet separated himself in his *mind* from those facts that nevertheless continued to claim a right over him; K. acts in the *closed* village, which determines his actions on all sides, without being able to justify his own presence. His *thing*, what seems to concern him essentially, truly rests on nothing. His history begins the moment when, after that long wait on the bridge, he decides to cross it; or rather, at the very moment when he is woken at the inn and told that the village belongs to the Schloss (and so he is, in some way, already 'staying or spending the

28 Kafka, *Castle*, p. 19.

night'[29] within it!) and will not be permitted to remain without the authorization of Count Westwest.

In the same way that he has *de-cided*[30] himself from his past, K. wishes to unlock the Schloss. He wants it with determination. He weighs up all the means necessary for the goal; he follows everything that is a useful sign or trail. If there is something that reveals his profession, it is this indefatigable calculating. But his calculation appears here 'without occupation'. It has no distance to cover nor land to measure. Nor are there doors to pull from their joints. Nobody prevents him from proceeding towards the Schloss; 'alone', it is as if the road drifted away. Nobody chases him away ('"Who would venture to throw you out, my dear sir"',[31] not even from the functionaries' apartments, nor from Klamm's carriage), but certainly no one is keeping him there. Neither did anyone chase him away or hold him back in his itinerary towards the castle. At each instant it was possible to become lost, at each moment to ruin the image of its stations by reducing them to mere obstacles to launch himself against. Is this the condition K. finds himself in? It is not he who 'had wanted to get into the castle [. . .] by night and unnoticed',[32] presuming to have been permitted access thanks to his own merits ('I don't want any tokens of favour from the Schloss, I want my rights [*sondern mein recht*]').[33]

K. is a complete stranger in this too, in being a stranger to all dimensions of faith. For this reason, theological Kafkaisms lack all

---

29 Kafka, *Castle*, p. 5.

30 Once again, Cacciari is highlighting that to 'decide' is etymologically linked to the Latinate *de* for 'off' and *caedere* 'to cut', so a decision here is a sort of caesura that, in deciding, separates from his past. [Trans.]

31 Kafka, *Castle*, p. 68.

32 Kafka, *Castle*, p. 31.

33 Kafka, *Castle*, p. 68.

foundation.[34] K. is in no way a self-portrait of Franz K., because the latter lived and wrote in the clear knowledge of not being able to be that Kierkegaard he so loved. The leap, the wager of faith is inconceivable for K. and impossible for Franz. But it is the latter who preserves within himself the *idea* of that castle whose heart can only be penetrated by the one who has traversed all its 'rooms' and who can ultimately overcome himself. K., on the other hand, leaves in the night, separated from everything, turning to others to know his path, demanding that his end be the 'prize' for his 'virtue'. Or rather: that achieving it represents the success, the full recognition of his being free. Favours offend him and he could not refuse an act of *grace*, simply because he would not even be aware of it.

But was he not *summoned*? Did he not go far from his birthplace, did he not 'exodus' because the Count sent for him? There is no documentation to that effect if not his own word, but only after he learns that the village belongs to the Count. He left everything (but, in truth, what does he remember?), without an invitation letter to

---

34 In particular, the reference to Job, which has become almost a *topos* of the more 'edifying' critical literature, is to my mind a complete red herring. K. is not tested, he is not 'dispossessed'. It is he who becomes lost. Job belongs firmly to a community and continues to belong to it even after calamity strikes him. He understands its language so well that he can 'take it apart', rationally, from within. K., on the other hand, remains a stranger to this language, and yet he would like for it to be transmitted in keeping with his capacity for listening. Job's aim is clear to him: to see face-to-face the God he has heard about. But he in no way doubts that the God he will see is the one he has heard about. K. knows nothing of Count Westwest and nothing is communicated to him. All *parousia* is excluded; and if even an End of the search exists, it lies in the most complete *apousia* or absence. (Of the literature on Kafka as a 'struggle with God', the most penetrating remains, to my mind, Margarete Susman's chapter 'Früheste Deutung Franz Kafkas' in *Gestalten und Kriese* [Stuttgart-Kostanz: Diana Verlag, 1954]).

show at the time of his first 'arrest'. And yet he shows that he places great store upon letters; *writing* is for him an object of special attention, as demonstrated by the attempted exegesis of the two letters that he receives from (possibly) Klamm. And yet Schwarzer does not ask him to provide a written invitation; it is as if such a thing is of no particular importance. In this fundamental scene, everything unfolds through oral communication. First, one of the understewards answers a question of clarification from Schwarzer with an absolute denial ('There's no record of any land surveyor')[35] and a moment later admits to the 'summons' (confirmed by the office manager himself!). But the revelatory, almost incidental passage, like a 'stolen letter', is the subsequent one, in which only at this point 'K. began to take notice. So the castle had appointed him land surveyor.' He's surprised. Was it that he'd taken a chance by calling himself a land surveyor, one whose consequences he could not predict? However, for him the *struggle* starts here. The Schloss accepted the challenge, it matters not whether he had provoked it or not. The Schloss knew 'all [it] needed to know' about K.—that he was or was not a land surveyor, that it had or had not summoned him. Does it perhaps think it holds him in its fist, in a state of permanent *terror*, '*in Schrencken*'? It is mistaken. The will that K. feels he possesses is, rather, ready to leverage that first concession so as to enter the world which he has entered. But he demands to be able to participate in it freely, which is to say, to know its reasons and his *own* within it.

There is no permit that K. can show that authorizes him to stay except for this *will* of his. He does not know where he is ('what village have I strayed into, then?').[36] He is only certain of having been on a long journey, of having to complete it *alone* to arrive at a place where to *remain*. This will must have been awakened by 'something'.

---

35 Kafka, *Castle*, p. 8.
36 Kafka, *Castle*, p. 5.

This 'cause' that separated him from everything, to the point of making him almost forget any past, is what he now wants to know, *to see face-to-face*. Is there a Lord of the place where his path has been interrupted, of that wretched village immersed in the snow? It is to him that he must turn, 'there's nothing else for it'. Through and *beyond* all the guards and custodians. Does that Lord live in the Schloss? So, he must *decide* to enter it, to 'open it'. This search, after an initial, brief 'indecision', is granted K.; he is free to attempt it. May his struggle begin. Is it that what he is summoned to? But summoned when, by whom? Summoned by himself, by the voice of his silence, forever *away* from his birthplace? However, it may be, now this is the essential need of his being-there: to be recognized. *You* summon me. It must be a You who summons, since it is only from a You that my freedom can be recognized. The trip could take place in solitude, but it cannot end in solitude. I do not *want it*. The will cannot merely want to-be-free [*l'essere-libero*]; freedom demands recognition from the other. And nobody could prevent it. K. struggles for this end as well. Not only does no one chase him away and no real barrier stands in his way but from the beginning he's treated with 'great courtesy'. That K. has arrived is *irreversible*. There is no 'authority' that could decide if he has really been summoned or not, but the very real 'scandal' is his presence in the here-and-now. Why is this stranger here? Why is he rather than is not? '*Sie sind nicht. Leider aber sind Sie*'. You are nothing and yet, unfortunately, you are something: a stranger, both to being and to non-being. A nothing that asks, that interrogates, that might even unsettle, disorient [*spaesare*].[37] A nothing that wants to know why he is. And who believes he may learn it from another, from whom he claims to have been personally

---

37 *Spaesare* means to disorientate, to leave without a country, without *paese* ('country'). The link to foreignness is embedded in the composition of the term itself. [Trans.]

summoned to carry out his own, peculiar, 'missions'. An extraordinary nothing (which is how he appears in Frieda's, Hans' and Peppi's eyes, of the 'youngsters' above all) in struggle for the *impossible.*

One speaks the impossible in many ways. The impossible coincidence of castle and Schloss; the impossible accord between the infinite road that leads to knowledge of 'who' calls at the base of the self on the one hand, and the mere interminability of the imperfect paths on the other. '[C]ould this walk go on forever, *unendlich?*',[38] K. asks, clinging tightly to Barnabas' arm, swearing to himself that nothing would deter him from '*weiter gehn*', from going on towards what he can only think of as a barred door. Is the road 'infinite' because it is not within K.'s 'powers' to complete it, or because to proceed along it would take an infinite duration? K. wants to 'press on'; but his pressing on in no way contains within it the sense of coming to an end, of completion. It is impossible that persisting in the time of the search and the struggle can, by its own strength, succeed in the 'happy' instant of the answer.

If the castle is a Schloss and establishes itself there, before us, as something that can only be unlocked, then to penetrate, to conquer it is impossible. K. is absolutely a stranger to, foreign to such an awareness. His question is always the same: 'Why is it impossible?'[39] He imagines that his liberty can be satisfied by reaching what he wants. But freedom can only '*weiter gehn*'; and pressing on can also always mean 'to have recourse'. The will certainly wants power, but it is 'thrown' into a world of facts that it did not want and that it always knows imperfectly. The will cannot even reveal how this initial gesture could have happened, one which made us presume our

---

38 Kafka, *Castle*, p. 29.
39 Kafka, *Castle*, p. 46.

being-free; the will that enabled K. to tear himself away, whether summoned or not, from his preceding state, so as to find himself alone in the night, in the fog, so as to *do* what he believes he is tasked to do. It is impossible that this idea of freedom coincides with the power to accomplish what one wishes. There is no question—K. is here, he has arrived. Those from the village have not moved at all, they have never 'travelled', and only Frieda appears to feel nostalgia for it. But K., the one who arrived *peregrinus*, through the snowy *ager*,[40] now would like to remain, 'to be', not 'to become'; he believes he has completed the journey that his being-free has 'mysteriously' allowed him. And now he advances the impossible pretence that his very freedom also guarantees that he can *remain*.

But his 'bare' remaining can only be permitted. Could they have not received him? The question is moot; the issue was decided with his very arrival. Not even the gods can *facta infecta fieri* [undo what has been done]. Nobody can drive K. away, because no one can turn back the arrow of time. But how can one infer from this that it is for one's freedom that one can 'continue' to the point of concluding, of *perficere* [complete] one's action, to the point of a 'happy' death?[41] Have you not read about the Prince of Denmark?

---

40 *Ager* is Latin for 'land', 'estate', 'territory'; *peregrinus* means 'foreigner, one from abroad'—it is related to the adverb *peregre* 'abroad', which is composed of *per-* (through) and *ager*. In Italian, 'land surveyor' is *agrimensore*, from the Latin *agrimensor*. [Trans.]

41 'The cruelty of death lies in the fact that it brings the real sorrow of the end, but not the end'; 'The greatest cruelty of death: an apparent end causes a real sorrow.' Franz Kafka, *The Blue Octavo Notebooks* (Ernst Kaiser and Eithne Wilkins trans, Max Brod ed.) (Cambridge, MA: Exact Change, 1991), p. 53. On this topic, which is also fundamental in Kafka, see Maurice Blanchot's 'Literature and the Right to Death' in *The Work of Fire* (Charlotte Mandel trans.) (Stanford, CA: Stanford University Press, 1995).

All of Kafka's 'parables' turn on such an *experience*: that life is *deviation*, that there is no path to *life*. To live is to set goals [*mète*], to desire them, but there is no perfect way leading to them. Each path is interrupted or goes astray. Every action is a letter destined for the always upcoming village, a word turned to the word that is lacking. This does not stem from a weakness of the will, from negligence or sloth, but from the fact that this life is infinite life, in itself incomplete, incapable both of proceeding to the infinite and of 'transfiguring itself' into an infinity in-itself, into true Life. There is a fragment in '"He": Notes from the Year 1920' where, in this respect, the entire elective affinity between Kafka and Wittgenstein is expressed: 'The bony structure of his own forehead blocks his way; he batters himself bloody against his own forehead'.[42] We find ourselves on the way, without being able clearly to indicate what makes this possible, the cause. But the path bifurcates at each moment. Each point along the way is that bridge upon which K. pauses before 'deciding' to take the path to the village. And from there begins the struggle to keep to the path—not simply to keep to it (a possibility that no one puts in doubt), but to give a complete meaning to that decision, to demonstrate its foundation—more, to demonstrate that it is the fruit of our being-free and that it will be upon this freedom that we shall construct here our abode.

And that is the *impossible*. It is impossible, first, to indicate the cause of the journey taken. Was K. moved by a nostalgia for going? Why then does he wish to 'interrupt' his destiny? Was that village his goal? Why then does he so obviously ignore its 'language'? Was he *summoned*? But if he was obeying an order, why insist on proclaiming his freedom? And, lastly, it is impossible that without answers to these questions, he can find an answer that is also a reason for life.

---

42 Franz Kafka, *Aphorisms* (Willa Muir, Edwin Muir and Michael Hofmann trans) (New York: Shocken, 2015), p. 112.

What's more, in K. there slowly grows the idea that 'the impossible proved to be impossible indeed (*sich das Unmöglich als unmöglich gezeigt hat*)',[43] and that his failures do not depend upon chance events, on the unreliability of the messengers, the hostility of the inhabitants, or the negligence of some of the functionaries. The idea of his own 'guilt' for the way he has approached the entire situation begins to make its way in him. 'Guilt' as radical lack and radical responsibility; 'guilt' as radical incapacity to respond to the 'desire' that has moved us, that has set us *en route*. No length of life would be sufficient to satisfy such a responsibility—and yet one lives for nothing but this. The impossible resists each and every 'demonstration' of its impossibility. Hence its nature is strictly that of the *indestructible*. The possible is what it is because it is actualized—but always imperfectly in comparison to its idea. The impossible, on the other hand, is the indestructible idea of true life, of happiness, without which it is even impossible to persist in living, and which no life can realize. It is necessary for it to be like this, because the impossible cannot be thought other than as the possible extreme, that 'possibility' which takes away[44] all others and is immanent to each. Immanent to each moment of life's incessant de-viation is the impossibility of reaching its End. The life that is dissipated among possibilities must safeguard that 'im-possible' that is the indestructible. It is the voice of the impossible that summons life and nourishes it in every action, even when it remains unheard, like the voice of compassion and forgiveness in Hamlet's action.

---

43 Kafka, *Castle*, p. 151.

44 See p. 42n15 in this volume.

K.'s errors are the signs of this 'guilt',[45] because K. is most certainly in error. And Kafka, who *recognizes* himself in him, represents him ruthlessly. K. is impatient, while his having been summoned should compel him to the most obedient waiting. K. misinterprets the importance of interrogation (in contrast to Kafka, who has learnt well—as he writes in Zürau—'I didn't understand why I got no answer to my question, today I don't understand how I presumed to ask a question').[46] K. is constantly inclined to hide the wretchedness of his state and overestimating the sense of his own freedom. K. falls into evident contradictions in his own attitude towards the world of the village, passing from moments of almost blind trust to others of incomprehension over the role that its inhabitants might play in the life of the Schloss. K. masks behind an expression of modesty the utterly unfounded demand that his rights and merits be recognized. It is not enough for him to have been summoned (if he indeed has been); he presumes he has been called for what he *can do*. Almost as if his *power* had imposed it. In this sense too, K. is as far from being an Abrahamic figure as Joyce's Ulysses is from being a Homeric character! But the most profound doubt corrodes K. regarding the basis of his questions and claims, and it grows in the course of events—the doubt that Kafka has been able to express in that extraordinary opening to the novel, where K. seems to discover where he finds himself and what he 'does' only through the words of Schwarzer and the under-stewards of the Schloss.

The error does not lie in his 'guilt', but in seeking in every way—unwittingly, at least until the end—to hide it from himself. However,

---

45 To forget that Kafka lived in a persistent state of 'guiltiness' is the worst possible error than can be committed in the 'exegesis' of his work. George Steiner understood this in his numerous contributions on the thought of this author.

46 Kafka, *Zürau Aphorisms*, p. 36.

it is only by *enduring* it with anguish that the idea of the inde-structible might *open* within us. Kafka learnt this from Kierkegaard, without being able to share in the experience of faith. This is what shows by way of negative contrast in K. For K., that the way might be *'unendlich'* signifies only delay and postponement; for him, the idea of the infinite only produces the anxiety of the interminable *'weiter gehn'*; the *próblema* forms itself in his eyes always in the guise of the obstacle, of the barred door—more still, of the *other* who 'envies' our *life*.

Kafka knows K.'s error intimately. And he knows that the Other—what we will in no way be able to 'capture', the im-possible—is nothing but the indestructible in us. Our own being-free holds no power over the indestructible im-possible—simply because it coincides with it. The indestructible that cannot be further grounded is nothing but the essence itself of being-there as freedom. Kafka signals this 'con-sciousness' through K.'s 'errancy'. One passage is particularly telling, when K. remains the 'only claimant to occupation of this place still left here'[47] in the courtyard of the Count's Arms, where he had waited, interminably, for Klamm's 'epiphany'. Having been 'abandoned', he becomes 'master'. He is allowed to do as he wishes since his doing can *decide* nothing. At this point, at this *turn* of events, K. intuits the aporia of the freedom that he thought he 'possessed'. He has finally been able to break all *Verbindung*, every connection with others; now he is free as never before; he has 'won', through his 'struggle' (*Erkampft*) such a freedom 'with more effort than most people could manage to make'.[48] A freedom, even an 'invulnerability'. And now this 'invulnerability' suddenly appears to him as senseless and desperate as anything could be. It was not to be free in this way that he had

---

47 Kafka, *Castle*, p. 94.
48 Kafka, *Castle*, p. 95.

fought but to be *recognized*. There can be no recognition through separating, remaining, and leaving 'in peace'. In this way Jacob becomes Israel: struggling *with* the angel. The invulnerable does not communicate and does not fight—it is the Closed, das Schloss. The idea of freedom 'alone' is turned into the image of the 'fortress' that K. wants to conquer.

A strange idea struck K.: that the Schloss had smilingly accepted the fight with him, having weighed up the balance of forces. How could the Schloss have any doubt concerning its heft when compared to K.? And why would it smile? The Schloss doesn't fight, it *withdraws*. What is closed cannot, at the same time, be open to struggle. What is *other* cannot be in struggle *with* K.; it 'smiles' at such an absurd presumption. 'Terror' does not seize K. due to the 'greatness' of the struggle he wants to wage, but because of the senselessness of the presumption. Hence the frightful image of an inoperative freedom. It is invulnerable because it is devoid of destination. You are free, writes Kafka in a posthumous fragment, and therefore you are lost.

Freedom lies only in its being recognized. But only by opening up to its own 'unfoundedness', only if it is affirmed as that which we cannot possess, can freedom open itself to the recognition of the other and to being recognized. If freedom 'closes' in on itself, no struggle is possible—only the obstinate and senseless continuing in itself, in the interminable search to make the content of its will *count* and in the illusion of being able to turn the other into a means. Hence, the interminability of the path will generate infinite fatigue. And the very 'chance', the narrow door, the eye of the needle—possibilities that, however improbable, cannot be excluded—will be eliminated precisely by the exhaustion that inevitably seizes those who have wagered everything on the accord between will, freedom and power. Only the opening onto the indestructible impossible would allow one, perhaps, to grasp, on one's way, the chance—*ex gratia*—were it to offer itself. But this form of decision-opening, *Ent-schlossenheit* is unknown to K. Nobody knows this better than Kafka, since no one more than he is alert to and suffers from the powerlessness to attain such a decision.

Is it through struggle and only through struggle that it is possible to be recognized, for our freedom to count and for its 'image' to be achieved? Yes—but only that struggle which opens *us* to recognition of that abyss of being-free and of the 'guilt' at being unable to respond to it, if not through imperfect paths and in the incompletion of our acting. But might we be *capable of*,[49] and not merely want, such an *Entschlossenheit*? No. Our decisions do not concern it; each decision remains in its area, but nobody 'decides' it. K.'s error consists instead in understanding it as that decision which unlocks the Other. His struggle, then, strains to make the Other into a *non*-Other; he would like for the Other to become 'combined' with himself in struggle, revealing to him the Name, and thus negating itself as such. An insuperable contradiction, and the downfall of K.'s path. And what is to be said to the one who rests, who waits upon his aporia—except to 'smile'? Who are we to struggle against? An enemy? But one does not ask an enemy for access. Even less does one ask that he respond to our will.[50] Do we struggle against the Other so that it finally reveals

---

49 In Italian, *potere* is both a noun, *il potere*, 'power', and a modal verb that in English is rendered either as 'can' or 'may'. *Potremmo* is a first-person plural conditional form of the verb *potere*, meaning 'we might' or 'we may'. Hence *potremmo potere* could be read as 'we might (*potremmo*) have the power to (*potere*)'. The English loses the etymological link present in the Italian. [Trans.]

50 K. thinks in term of the 'struggle for recognition'. That means thinking that recognition of one's Self must necessarily pass by way of a struggle with the other. And yet Kafka could never have written a novel entitled *The Enemy*, as Carl Schmitt instead wanted to, and for precisely the reasons that

itself? In that case, it cannot be understood as Schloss. Against oneself? So as to open oneself to an idea of freedom that no one has 'made', which is neither merit nor right, which is simply the 'indestructible' to which it is impossible to correspond completely and before which we are 'guilty'? But K. always *errs* in the face of this question, from which he tears himself away even in those moments when Kafka appears to address it to him most painfully. His interpreting and interrogating represent instead the question's displacement.

Is K. 'abandoned' to his freedom because he cannot see its essence? Because he does not understand that the essence of decision lies in opening himself? Because he is always 'undecided' between the 'abstract' claim of autonomy and the assertion of his being-summoned? These are the terms in which Kafka outlines K's character-daemon. But with 'fear and trembling' he also tells us that nothing, at least nothing in this world, still calls to mind the idea of the castle. Just as the form of prayer has contracted in K. into that of exacting questioning, so too is his path reduced to an interest in the mere goal, so that nothing in the 'landscape' that surrounds him contains even the ruin of the symbol of the castle. If there are no barriers, if one doesn't run into barred doors, if no one prevents one from 'wandering' all over the place, it is because at this point all distance has become a matter of indifference. K. loses himself in this indifference. Never would his mind have recognized the symbol of the castle, and yet he is not wrong in refusing to give this name to the place where he would like to live and where instead he is only allowed to survive. He's not Jacob K. In any case, it is an inconceivable and

Schmitt gives: the enemy can never be clearly defined, 'measured', for Kafka. It is not the enemy who provokes anxiety, but rather precisely the absence of the enemy's real 'face'. See Carl Schmitt, *Glossario* (Petra Dal Santo ed.) (Milan: Giuffrè, 2001), p. 52.

even un-hoped-for possibility that a 'being' might appear who could fight with him. Nobody struggles with K. to tear him from his idea of freedom. Nobody has summoned him to this struggle; however much K. shows he has desired it. He in turn only knows how to call the one who by definition would never be able to reply—a fact that all the 'intermediaries' invite him to recognize.

The world in which he finds himself appears to K. compact but of porous consistency, full of crevices, holes, interstices, where the 'exception' can always lie in wait. K. tries to leverage these exceptions to open a path for himself. Bloch saw in Kafka's world the merging of ancient forgotten norms, harking back to the time that preceded the prophetic rationalization of the Law, with an epoch still to come, filled with unpredictable possibilities and threats.[51] It seems to me that in *Das Schloss,* we see how that process of rationalization is able to reach its zenith, becoming entirely 'autonomous', completely self-referential, and how it becomes *impossible* to justify for the subject that interrogates it. The voids that compose its structure open up only where the sense of the question itself crumbles away. Together, Schloss and Dorf demonstrate in practice the very real paradox of a *communitas* that wants to reproduce itself as perfectly *immune*.

The world of the Schloss has no 'holes' other than the exhaustion which inevitably assails those who presume to 'open it'. As we have seen, the 'complicity' of Schloss and Dorf is almost perfect. He who does not belong to it is automatically a stranger, even if he continues to reside in their 'system'. The stranger 'senses' the stranger, as is the case between K. and Amalia, but among strangers no true alliance can form. What alternative law might such an alliance affirm? And against whom? K. judges what happened to Amalia to be entirely

---

51 Ernst Bloch, *Heritage of Our Times* (Neville and Stephen Plaice trans) (Cambridge: Polity Press, 1991), p. 222.

unjust. But Olga explains that her sister has not been accused of anything and no tribunal has condemned her. Nor has she been called to trial. Those who 'exceed' the unwritten 'constitution' of the Schloss exclude themselves. Naturally, lacking any accusation of guilt, it will also be impossible to prove one's innocence. And it is senseless to implore forgiveness or show repentance. The 'integral' complicity of the different dimensions of this world, having become a form of life—an *ethos* in the most originary sense of the term—does not entertain the possibility of a 'state of exception' or of an event that *decides* it, but only that there be those who do not understand that *ethos*, who are unable to internalize it. Nevertheless, there will be no need to 'repress' the *individual* who dreams of being able to impose her own universal, personal language, since she will be unable to communicate with anyone, since her 'concerns' will be entirely incomprehensible. The immanence of law in the life of everyone becomes evident where there 'happen' to be those who presume freely to correspond to it, to conceive law as the 'product' of their freedom.

But the extraordinariness of this world (which is equally the extraordinariness of Kafka's writing) is that such compactness is inhabited by hybrid, changeable, ungraspable figures, by an apparently chaotic ensemble of actions and reactions, orders and counterorders. Its unity is indisputable and yet doubles continually. It is an Order, and yet *insecurus*; *invulnerable*, and yet personified by characters who move as if constantly menaced. At some point, this is put down to their timidity. The real reason, which is essential for understanding the novel, is given by Burgel in his night-time monologue. The solidity of this Order is founded upon nothing, just like K.'s hopes. Since its foundation is simply 'indisputable', it is impossible to foresee or know anything concerning its future (and hence also about K.'s 'cause'). Its apparent immobility is, therefore, that which 'comes to a halt' before the 'everything is possible'. A state without memory 'assures' that it is necessary that it be thus and so, no other possibility would be 'logically' obtainable from the naked *fact* that this Order is given. Yet the impossible is nothing but the extremity of the possible. And the febrile, sleepless exertion of the administrators and functionaries, the sheer quantity of actions, the length of the procedures, the 'illegibility' of the laws, all of this serves to make us forget, remove, and cancel it. To exhaust the search for the Order.

There is no middle ground between Dorf and Schloss, neither temporal nor spatial, but only convergent points of view to indicate the same essence. It is K. who fails to understand it, as if 'bewitched' by a theology of the absolutely Other.[52] But the Other has become entirely 'incarnated', thus annulling all distance. 'Everything gets lumped into uniform distancelessness [*Abstandlose*]'[53] says Heidegger—which appears to be a comment on *Das Schloss*. Even the Sovereign is missing, or that Form which contains everyone within it, and which was already displayed by Hamlet at the start of his ruin. 'Sovereignty' is at work immediately in everyone. Its artifice has become neo-nature. The system requires no *subject* in order to function. Jünger and Schmitt call it *Führung ohne Führer*. Command

---

52 'Kafka thus becomes not a proponent of dialectical theology, as is often asserted, but its accuser. Its "absolute difference" converges with the mythic powers.' Theodor W. Adorno, *Prisms* (Shierry Weber Nicholsen and Samuel Weber trans) (Cambridge, MA: MIT Press, 1967), p. 268. I think that Adorno is wrong in his interpretation of dialectical theology, but right in understanding Kafka outside of a theology of the absolutely Other. [The Italian translation Cacciari provides differs somewhat from the English. The former might be rendered as follows: 'Kafka becomes the accuser of dialectical theology, into which he is wrongly situated. The God of the latter, as the absolutely different, converges with mythic forces.'—Trans.]

53 Martin Heidegger, 'The Thing' in *Poetry, Language, Thought* (Albert Hofstadter trans.) (New York: Harper and Row, 1971), p. 166.

without a Who.[54] There is no guide, even less are there shepherd gods. The King's body has been 'taken on' by everyone. This does not exclude the eventuality of disobedience but renders it inefficacious to the point of senselessness. To disobey would be not to recognize one's own sovereignty.[55]

This helps one to understand the tragic irony of insisting so much on K.'s occupation: *Landervermesser* [land-surveyor]. He was supposed to measure distances where there are none! The Schloss is not at all 'distant'. Nothing is distant and nothing nearby. Moreover, these distances that do not exist are supposed to be measured by a stranger, by someone without land and who does not know the one he is in! In Latin, the word for land-surveyor is *metator*, and it seems that it is precisely from that name that one derives the name of the great angel Metatron, who plays such a great role in apocalyptic literature and in Jewish mysticism, as the custodian-revealer of the utmost secrets of the Throne.[56] Is it the angel who has fallen into the Schloss, forgetful of its heights, and who must measure the incalculable distance that separates this world from Revelation? Here the bare fact reigns within an immanence that truly cannot be transcended. In the Schloss, there are no closed doors because none give

---

54 This might be best summarized as 'command without s/he who commands', or more literally, 'leadership without a leader'. [Trans.]

55 *The Castle* can in no way be read in terms of the opposition between the 'offended and humiliated' and power, or between subjects and sovereign. The Power of the Schloss in its indeterminacy and, at the same time, its extremely determinate *complicity* with the village, can in no way be fitted into a traditional 'political theology', nor into the phenomenology of Elias Canetti's masterpiece, *Crowds and Power*.

56 For innumerable suggestions and research ideas, I am indebted to Moshe Idel's investigations into Jewish mysticism and messianic themes, where the name Kafka recurs in many important passages. See his *Messianic Mystics* (New Haven, CT: Yale University Press, 1998).

onto 'the open'. The need to 'accomplish' the path of life can only be expressed via 'infinite demands'.[57]

Nonetheless, what appears to be in-itself perfectly closed is not at all 'totally' so. Even if K. does not understand the nature of the Schloss in its relation to the village, even if his impatience renders it a priori impossible to grasp the occasion, were it to present itself, it remains a fact that the system into which he has 'fallen' will never be able to annul the ocean of unpredictability that embraces him. The inhabitants of the Schloss are ignorant of all this, but they cannot stop their features, gestures and behaviours from constantly displaying the *insecuritas* that derives from this. He who conserves the Closure on

---

57 'What we are is reflected

    In endless instances [*in unendlichen Instanzen*].

    Nobody knows the way completely

    And each part of it makes us blind.

    No one can benefit from redemption [*Erlösung*] [the reference to

        the *Star of Redemption* by Franz Rosenzweig is evident].

    That star stands far too high.

    And if you had arrived there too,

    You would still stand in your way.'

(The same can be found in Kafka: 'He has the feeling that merely by being alive he is blocking his own way. From this sense of hindrance, in turn, he deduces the proof that he is alive' [*The Great Wall of China* (Willa and Edwin Muir trans) (New York: Schocken Books, 1970), p. 154]). These are the words of Gershom Scholem in a poem that accompanied a letter and *The Trial*, which he sent to Walter Benjamin on 9 July 1934. [See *The Correspondence of Walter Benjamin and Gershom Scholem 1932–1940* (Gershom Scholem ed., Gary Smith and Andre Lefevere trans) (New York: Schocken Books, 1989), p. 124. —Trans.] Alongside Benjamin's great essay for the tenth anniversary of Kafka's death, the correspondence between the two, precisely in their radical contradiction, constitutes the highest introduction to his work.

'incalculable' foundations is condemned to a senseless and exhausting labour. A labour that is tantamount to being 'occupied', destined for nothing, analogous to the one that K. is expected to 'content' himself with. The functionaries of the Schloss express the world of action's impotence at its extreme point; they express the world of the impossibility of *deciding* at its 'perfect' level. That K. wants to do what he has been summoned to do, appears, in this world, an incomprehensible scandal.

Like Hamlet, K. too acts, incites himself to action, seeking its motives. But the power to decide has become the hallmark of the impossible itself. Hamlet's actions took place in the context of a common language, which he showed he knew at the same time that he experienced its intolerableness. K., however, is pure *individual*; he has lost 'his own' for a summons that he alone *demands*. He doesn't know how to wait; he seeks, to the point of inevitable exhaustion. This alone can he 'decide': to resist where he finds himself, transforming into a 'necessity' what has all the appearances of contingency. 'Undecided' between one interpretation and another, one intermediary and another, between, the condition of the stranger, perhaps living in the house of the 'excluded', and, resigning himself to not-knowing, happy only with his 'invulnerability', K.'s actions cannot even find that 'unsatisfactory' 'completion' that is represented for Hamlet by revenge. The voids of the Schloss swallow all demands or needs and reduce every action to mere tarrying.[58]

Hamlet's acting is extinguished in the actions he has not decided, since it cannot correspond to the essential contents of his will. The action separated itself from the character-daemon of the hero. K.'s acting extinguishes itself in exhaustion, which is not the renunciation of action but the expression of the manifest powerlessness to bring

---

58 'Tarrying' here translates the noun *indugio*, from the verb *indugiare*, 'to tarry', 'to delay', 'to hesitate', 'to procrastinate'. [Trans.]

its meaning to 'conclusion'. Hamlet 'seeks' the delay and ultimately surrenders by obeying the concatenation of facts that will bring him to that conclusion of which he was in no way 'convinced'. K. surrenders? It is possible to think this, and that Kafka had thought so is demonstrated by certain sketches for the novel's development. But essentially what is revealed in K. is the impossibility of arriving at any authentic decision. Here Hamlet's 'end' falls as well, since to choose is nothing but the expression of freedom aiming to be the essence of the will of being-there. K. wants to be summoned, but he is not needed. His doing is almost-nothing. The freedom that appeared to determine him is absolutely inessential. That which is the essence of being-there sinks into the most complete inessentiality.

This is the condition of indecision and suspension described in many places by Kafka. We do not have access to the tree of life, to 'rest' in the accomplished life. Our expulsion from Paradise is eternal; and yet, precisely because it is eternal, because it does not belong to our becoming, it will also be possible to affirm that we remain within it always. Eternally in Paradise in the instant we are expelled from it. Eternally separated and eternally in contact with that life. 'From this region there is simply no way to life', but it is certain that 'there must have been a way from life' that can be imagined to exist and that leads here.[59] We have lost the way from that path, but our having gone astray cannot mean that that life is nothing. For this living to be fulfilled, we should not have nourished ourselves solely at the tree of judgement, of the *krisis*,[60] but at that of life. Only if we were able to,

59 Franz Kafka, *A Hunger Artist and Other Stories* (Joyce Crick trans.) (Oxford: Oxford University Press, 2012), p. 208.

60 *Krinein* is the present active infinitive of the ancient Greek verb *krínō*, which means, *inter alia*, 'to separate', 'to divide', 'to decide', 'to accuse' and 'to judge'. Cacciari has long meditated on the relationship between crisis, decision and judgement, not least in his *Krisis. Saggio sulla crisi del pensiero negativo da Nietzsche a Wittgenstein* (Milan: Feltrinelli, 1976). [Trans.]

would we really know and would our actions be well-founded. At present we lack the strength for this. The exhausting search for motivations, for 'grounds',[61] expresses nothing but the impossibility of comprehending the aim of action. Since here is where we find ourselves, there *must* be a reason; if we've arrived here through one path or another, we must seek out the motives. If someone or some thing has summoned us, we must seek out its name. The 'invention' of motives becomes the only possible form of knowledge, a pale 'substitute' of the End that no action and no writing can arrive at. This is the Kafka of the third of *The Blue Octavo Notebooks*, the final fragments of 'He', and the most Hamletic of the Zürau aphorisms.

    '*Ich will immer frei sein*': K. introduces himself with these words. This will to freedom (to affirm freedom as the essence of will) crumbles in the night spent with Burgel at the Count's Hotel. The freedom that K. has available to him is a freedom that judges, divides, plans, 'invents' its motivations, but he is unable to find the path that leads from this world to life. The idea of freedom that K. manifests as though it were his most intimate *possession* is essentially 'unfit' for this task. And yet it is endowed with a 'weak messianic power'[62]— one that expresses itself in its necessarily critical-negative dimension. The experience of the stranger K. not only demonstrates the insuperable limit of freedom conceived of as the product of the will—as a 'thing' that is ours—but the crisis of a community, a world, an order of discourse that has 'closed' within itself the ek-static idea of the freedom of being-there.[63] K. is unable to free himself of this

---

61 In English in the original. [Trans.]
62 Walter Benjamin, 'On the Concept of History' (Harry Zohn trans.) in *Selected Writings, Volume 4: 1939–40* (Howard Eiland and Michael W. Jennings eds) (Cambridge, MA: Belknap Press, 2003), p. 390. [Trans.]
63 Cacciari is here playing with the Heideggerian term of *Ekstase* of temporality discussed on p. 38n7 in this volume. We see here how the Schloss

world-not-life; the freedom he 'defends' would never allow him to; nevertheless, and this is precisely what his whole tale demonstrates, right upto his 'collapse', he leaves 'involuntarily' open the instance of the 'true' Messiah. When there will be no more Hamlets nor K.'s, then there will no longer be even the need for a Messiah. If the Hamlets and the K.'s all end on the last day, the Messiah will arrive at the very last one—when no one will believe in him, for to 'believe' (*glauben*) means 'freeing' (*befreien*) the indestructible within oneself, or rather: being indestructible, or, better still, *being* (as in the third of *The Blue Octavo Notebooks*, 30 November 1917).[64] The Messiah will come when no one asks themselves if there is a path that can lead from this zone to life. The Messiah will come when he 'knows' how to be a perfect stranger. A stranger like K.

The story could perhaps also be told differently. As we are *always* expelled from Paradise, 'undecided' on the scene, in the same way the Messiah has come and always comes. But, each time, in order to liberate, he is forced to 'enter' into that which must be liberated. And how might he have access to the unredeemed world if he did not have the keys? If his annunciation were solely to be that of the Other? How could he triumph over [*super-vincere*] Evil if he did not know it was within him? To free us, he must burst into the darkness and fog of the Schloss, and thus to have always *endured* an essential bond

---

'closes' what, within the primordial temporality of the ek-stases of authentic freedom, is a 'standing outside' itself. Whereas the *'existential-temporal conditions for the possibility of the world* [a horizon of meaning and meaningful action] *lies in the fact that temporality, as an ecstatical unity, has something like a horizon'*—the closure of that 'horizon' at one stroke denies the possibility of meaningful action. Heidegger, *Being and Time*, p. 416 (emphasis in the original). [Trans.]

64 Kafka, *The Blue Octavo Notebooks*, p. 27.

with it. To announce the path that leads out of Hamlet's prison, and from K.'s Schloss, the Messiah returns (or is he sent? by a 'good' Father, perhaps struggling against a 'jealous' alter-Ego, or with himself?)—and he is forced into this by the 'logic' of his figure, even in its philosophical versions, the 'secularized' ones from Plato to Nietzsche's Zarathustra. Can K. be understood as the contradictory, feeble sign of the listening for that annunciation? Can his very failure be seen as the awakening of the prisoner to the awareness of his wretchedness? Or does *Das Schloss* express the following sentence: let no one await the one who frees; even those who wait know not what they await? The Saviour can no longer be saved. And so the word passes to Beckett.

Alternatively: in this Schloss, in which power subsumes all distance, in this hell of the *Abstandlose*, the distanceless, where one is a prisoner of chains that allow one to *stray* [*errare*] everywhere, except towards the earth or the sky, towards the highest things—here the Messiah has fallen with us. He has come, he has been unable to free us, and he too has found himself chained so tightly as to be unable to flee. The husks, the 'nutshells', he was there to break have captured him. There is nothing left to wait for, because he is—true presence— but in the hell of this life–non-life. Therefore, the need for him will never end, just as it will never be satisfied. The desire for the Messiah represents the impossible—that his coming could be what it was not: victorious. Hence it is perhaps another sign of our straying to say that he will come, but when there will no longer be any need for him. He has come, he is here, and under the sign of his unredeemable defeat he must continue to be awaited and to inspire our need.

THREE

After the Last Day

In one of his *Récits en rêve* (Dream tales), Yves Bonnefoy imagines the artist of the final day. 'The world was about to end' since 'the set of images produced by humanity would have surpassed the number of living creatures'. The equilibrium between the *life* and the *appearance* of signs was breaking down forever. The images were about to realize their destiny: to submerge life, transposing the world into the multiverse of the languages that claim to signify and possess it. The artist of the final day is conscious of it and stays his hand. His work thus tends to become a kind of tarrying. He *seeks*. His work becomes an experimenting. But the delay in *experiri* is unable to last eternally, if not by transforming itself into an end and so denying itself. The awaiting of the decision remains within the horizon of decision and is nourished by the idea of decision. Upon the artist of the last day looms the necessity of choice: either 'purify' the image to the point that, ceasing to be the 'illicit rival of that which exists', it appears in itself as world, or 'extinguish all sources of light' and lead all words to perfect silence.[1]

But might this bifurcation not be merely apparent? How could the image of the tree be at one with the *life* of the tree? Vice versa, how can the most abstract of images, the most 'autonomous' poetic world,

---

1 Yves Bonnefoy, *Racconti in sogno* (Cesare Greppi trans.) (Milan: Egea, 1992), pp. 100–103.

not suggest something 'real' or a lived event? Is not 'extinguishing the light' also a gesture, a form of doing, a representation of the disquiet and *insecuritas* inherent in the world of images? Hence, this world must end. The 'real' world is already finished; now its 'illicit rival' must end as well. And it is the task of the writer of the last day to 'put an end to this'. And then? Will the echo of the writer's 'decision' continue infinitely? Will nostalgia for the signs and images that his gesture appeared to have submerged prevail? Will the nauseating play of representations be revived, perhaps in the desecrating form of irony?

Beckett is situated on the meridian of these questions—*beyond* the artist of the last day. And for him this means beyond Joyce. 'Beyond' [*oltre*] here sounds like the exact opposite of 'overcoming' [*oltrepassare*]. The 'wave-like agitation of words'[2] has *crashed* against the great scene of *Ulysses*. Now it is only possible to proceed by *retreating*. It is the age of the great undertow, leaving strewn across the beach *disjecta membra*, unrecognizable and irredeemable fragments. The world that was has passed along with the words that were images of it, that 'betrayed' it in images. It is no longer representable—and words must express its unrepresentability to the point of being transformed into voices, fragments of voices, sounds more than voices, gestures more the sounds. The naked body of those unnameable things, torn from all *discourse*. This is a paradoxical overturning of the cabalistic *tzimtzum*. There, God 'retreats' into the supra-essential No-thing so that the thing may be, so as to give way to the thing; it is a 'retreat' that creates, a productive retreat. Here, on the other hand, the same power of the *Verbum* is seen as the energy that silences, that destines to silence.

---

2 Georges Bataille, 'Molloy's Silence' in *On Beckett: Essays and Criticism* (S. E. Gontarski ed.) (London: Anthem Press, 2014), p. 104.

Discourse. Dual word. First used in the well-connected and founded sense of judging, of a computing that *compels* to persuasion. This meaning echoes, for instance, in the German *Rede* (*ratio, reor, ratus sum*: what is in vain, does not count or counts for so little that it cannot be 'computed'). But the term 'discourse' indicates, within its very etymology, a completely different condition, opposed to that of *Rede*: the condition of *dis-currere*, of running hither and thither, going while scattering itself, proceeding in disarray. Now, for Beckett, after Joyce, both senses of 'discourse' appear *out of use*, both the *Rede* and its simple reversal in *dis-currere*. Beckett's writing is a perennial, inexhaustible struggle against the dis-course into which we are immersed, a perennial ascesis towards being able to *un-say* through its own implacable representation.

One can understand Beckett only by beginning with his essay, published in 1929 by Shakespeare & Co., 'Dante . . . Bruno . Vico . . Joyce' (the periods indicate the centuries separating the writers from one another). Joyce is the *last* because he has perfectly understood that words are not 'mere polite symbols'[3] but must ultimately coincide with what they express. That is, they must 'know' that of which they speak, in the same way that Shakespeare uses 'fat, greasy' words to represent decay, and terms that *are* sludge or bog to indicate the rotten. The word must live for itself, elbow its way forward, glow, flare up or fade to the point of exhaustion. The different situations should be not 'staged' by the word but should be the word itself. This confers upon form that 'furious restlessness'[4] which constitutes

---

3 Samuel Beckett, 'Dante . . . Bruno . Vico . . Joyce' in Samuel Beckett et al., *James Joyce, Finnegans Wake—A Symposium: Our Exagmination Round his Factifcation for Incamination of Work in Progress* (Paris: Shakespeare & Co., 1929; New York: New Directions, 1972 [facsimile edn]), p. 14.

4 Beckett, 'Dante . . . Bruno . Vico . . Joyce', p. 16.

Joyce's secret and which he supposedly learnt from his great Italians. The heroic frenzy of the word itself. The tectonic power of the poem that gushes forth from the voice of Vico's 'big beast', from the original cry, which is all-of-a piece with the astonishment and terror aroused by the 'spectacle' of the *thing*, by its being-against-us, *Gegenstand*,[5] inescapable *pròblema*, pre-possessing[6] all our 'diction'. It is by excavating the etymology of the word, listening to all the resonances of their different idioms, that we find the traces of their origin, preceding all *discourse*, and, at the same time, perhaps, the clues to their end . . . Within the word is expressed that same *physis* that loved 'to hide itself', *natura*, future participle, perennial germination.

But all this evokes a beyond of writing. How then, after Joyce, can one exhibit in the word itself, *immediately* within it, to the thing's doing-undoing? Won't we ultimately fall into mere repetition? Into the boredom of the duration of the already-done? Indeed, what word could be 'left over'[7] in the wake of the germinating omni-

---

5 The word *Gegenstand*, a common word for 'object' in German, is made up of two elements: *gegen-*, 'opposed' or 'against', and *stand*, 'to be' or 'to stand'. Hence the object or thing, *Gegenstand*, can also be understood in terms of a 'standing/being-against'. [Trans.]

6 Cacciari's *pre-potente* defies translation. Playing here with the Italian word, *prepotente*, usually translated as 'overbearing', Cacciari's hyphenation (*pre-potente*) emphasizes the etymology of the component elements of the word: 'pre-', gives a temporal dimension of 'before', whereas the isolation of this lexical element from the latter, *potente*, 'to have power', makes the link to power explicit. I have opted for 'pre-possessing' and 'pre-possession' (in the following paragraph) because it retains the temporal moment as well as an etymological link to power, although the issue is not here one of property and ownership but of power and control. [Trans.]

7 *Avanzare* can mean both 'to advance' and 'to be left over', 'to be in excess of'. Cacciari is drawing upon this ambiguity. [Trans.]

compossibility that is expressed in the word of Joyce (the *catholic* coincidence of opposites, orthodoxy–heresy, blasphemy–praise)?[8] Certainly, no *literary* word. What is left is the renunciation of that word. What is left over after the great tidal wave that has shattered all words is the undertow and what it de-poses. After imposition, naked deposition. After the word capable of recreating the original pre-possession of the thing itself, the *poverty* of those beached wrecks, the 'word' of the unnameable. After the search and 'futuring' [*infuturanti*] experimentation, the vanity of the wait—since with Joyce the last day has passed.

Joyce could not prevent it. He demonstrates what Vico knew: the abyssal power of the word. But no word is enough to arrest the 'foul river' of images. Joyce marks their outlet. And then? Then it will no longer be the time of images, the epoch in which being-there manifests itself in the *dis-coursing*[9] of representations, the time we measure by the rhythm of the coming and going from and into nothing. There will no longer be time. The word that 'is left over' for Joyce cannot be understood differently: it is *atemporal*.[10] It relinquishes the 'dream'

---

8 As Beckett states in a *New York Times* interview of 1956: '[Joyce is] tending towards omniscience and omnipotence as an artist. I'm working with impotence, ignorance . . . There seems to be a kind of aesthetic axiom that expression is an achievement—must be an achievement. My little exploration is that whole zone of being that has always been set aside by artists as something unusable—as something by definition incompatible with art.' 'Beckett: Moody Man of Letters', *The New York Times* (6 May 1956), p. 3.

9 The hyphenation that Cacciari again introduces into the common word *discorrere*, *dis-correre*, draws attention to a word that can mean 'to run to and fro' as well as 'to discuss' or 'expound upon' something, thus drawing together the image of the 'foul river' as well as the issue of 'the word' central to this paragraph. [Trans.]

10 Günther Anders dedicates a part of his *Die Antiquiertheit des Menschen* [The obsolescence of man] to Beckett, precisely on this fundamental aspect

of being able to say something beyond its emptying itself and, at the same time, incarnating itself in the 'misery' of those indecipherable fragments that survived the end of the world. It is a word he *does not have*. For Beckett, to write after Joyce means much more than noting the end of Europe's literary adventure, the completion and exhaustion of its great wave. It means daring the impossible: to *imagine* again, after the last artist, the last *poietés*, the highest of the 'greatest smithies'. But what out of inner necessity comes to be placed in an image is nothing other than the self-same *im-potence* 'left' by the wave once it has retreated. Our word must *be* this impotence, just as the 'furious restlessness' of Joycean form *was* multiform, ungraspable *physis*.

On the beach lie the dismantled remains of the great representation and of the will that was at one with it. Even to survive in their memory would be nothing but a museum-like mourning, it would be nothing but a masking, through the veneration of the world-of-literature, of the fact that we must work by means of impotence. The final works have already desecrated this idolatry; they have been able to gather the great legacy of the past precisely by 'completing it'. All else will be nothing but *religio* for *religare*, not even for *re-legere*, which would mean to comprehend, gather, interiorize—and perfectly digest.[11] That age has definitively passed. To draw on another image

---

of his work, specifically in *Waiting for Godot*. It is clear that 'atemporal' also means 'without death'. And so returns the *basso continuo* of *Hamlet* and Kafka. [Only extracts of Anders' book exist in English; fortunately, among these is the essay 'Being Without Time: On Beckett's Play *Waiting for Godot*' in Martin Esslin (ed.), *Samuel Beckett: A Collection of Critical Essays* (Prentice-Hall, NJ: Englewood Cliffs, 1965). —Trans.]

11 There is a useful account of the Latin roots to which Cacciari draws our attention in a brief article by Benson Saler: 'the scholarly literature directs

of Bataille's: the castle that the last artist has erected cannot be further transformed so that it may be inhabited: its 'wide-open windows allow wind and rain to enter'.[12] Those fated to come *afterwards* will be forced to work with 'ruins' such as these.

This is a recoil against all forms of 'will to power,' which is nevertheless inscribed in the latter's history. The will to power cannot 'complete itself' except by willing against itself, by willing *power* against itself. In the end, its 'long duration' generates boredom, the desire for ruin. But it is not a desire that aspires to anything else or presages it; rather, it is the corrosion of all forms, the irony that sees in the rising up of all forms the *facies* of the wreckage. This 'supreme irony' still belongs to the artist of the last day, the one who dismantles the will to power of the *I*. To those forced to work after him (unable not to do so, because their *body* demands it) nothing remains but the exposition of naked wreckage in the language of pure impotence.[13]

---

our attention to two candidates from which *religio* may have derived: *legere*, "to gather together", "to arrange", a proposed derivation that we associate with Cicero, and *ligare*, "to tie together", "to bind", a possibility entertained by Lucretius and favored by the Christian writers, Lactantius and Tertullian.' See 'Religio and the Definition of Religion', *Cultural Anthropology* 2(3) (1987): 395–99. [Trans.]

12 Bataille, 'Molloy's Silence', p. 105. [Translation modified; the extant English translation reads rather differently: 'empty mansions left to the gentle mercy of the wind and rain'. —Trans.]

13 In a posthumous fragment, Kafka writes: 'Some object or other from a shipwreck, which was new and beautiful when it went into the water, soaked and made defenceless for years on end, *finally undone*.' Franz Kafka, 'Fragments from Note-Books and Loose Pages' in *Wedding Preparations in the Country and Other Posthumous Prose Writings* (Ernst Kaiser and Eithne Wilkins trans) (London: Secker and Warburg, 1954), p. 298 [translation modified; Cacciari's emphasis].

But that such a language is *pure*; that it should erase everything inessential; that it appears as a 'methodical ascesis'[14]—here is where there appears to arise an imperious duty-*Sollen*, a desire for 'poverty' that truly borders mystical 'nudity'. That such a language truly be emptied of all elements of representation, comprehension, acquisition. That the word be *deletion* or 'drops of silence' (*The Unnamable*);[15] that it not be mere 'intention' to the desert but that it exposes it and 'cares' for it; that it not preach its distance from the *iconodulia* of the world of representation, but instead turns it into the flesh, the nerves, the gestures of its figures. Never add! This is the imperative that in the final works of Beckett becomes almost obsessional. 'Say for be said. Somehow on', as if to say 'Fail worse again',[16] to go ('No. No out. No back. Only in.')[17] towards the 'worst'—where 'worst' [*pessimo*] should be understood etymologically: *pessum dare* means to make fall; *pessum ire* means to ruin. To 'worsen', 'to go' towards the 'worst' therefore, in this context, counts as 'lessening' all to a zero point, where the very 'dim' goes, '[f]or worst and all',[18] like a failing (falling, emptying itself) to the point of the 'unlessenable least'[19]—unlessenable because the absolutely nothing remains absolutely unsayable. It is

14 Alain Badiou, *On Beckett* (Nina Power and Alberto Toscano trans and eds) (Manchester: Clinamen Press, 2003), p. 45.

15 Samuel Beckett, *The Unnamable* (New York: Grove Press, 1978), p. 133.

16 Samuel Beckett, *Worstward Ho* in *Nohow On: Company, Ill Seen Ill Said, and Worstward Ho* (London: John Calder, 1992), pp. 101, 102. [Cacciari draws on Gabriele Frasca's Italian translation of the text as *Peggio tutta* in Samuel Beckett, *In nessun modo ancora* (Gabriele Frasca ed.) (Turin: Einaudi, 2008), pp. 66–87.—Trans].

17 This is phrase is the closest to the Italian translation, which more literally would read: 'No. No goings. No returns. Only being' (*No. Niente andate. Niente ritorni. Solo esservi*). [Trans.]

18 Beckett, *Worstward Ho*, p. 113.

19 Beckett, *Worstward Ho*, p. 103. [Trans.]

possible only to 'worsen', but there is no *henosis* with the Worst.[20] The 'worse' word always represents its distance or nostalgia towards the Worst. Yes, as Cioran understood, in the distant background there always stands Meister Eckhart, the 'noble man',[21] but also the 'hidden' Eckhartian Nietzsche who reveals himself in the idea of the Over-man. Albeit with an abyssal difference: the noble man leaves everything in order to 'enter into God' [*indiarsi*] and become one with the very Beginning; Beckett re-leases all will-to-power so as to appear 'unsavable' in his wretchedness. In the mystical, one retraces creation's path backwards to arrive at the initial Indifference, the one between the creator and the creature. In Beckett, de-creation is the dis-integration of all connection, harmony, discourse. It expresses nothing but the becoming unnameable of every origin and every destiny.

It is not even possible to speak a destiny of death. Croaking is not dying, as we have already heard from Hamlet and from K. Hamlet's terror does not consist in the unknown 'something' after death but in the fear of an apparent end—an end that does not free one from surviving. This 'eternal' ending ('The zenith. Evening again. When not night it will be evening. Death again of deathless day' [*Immortel jour qui agonise encore*])[22] is the only 'remainder' after the last day. The word becomes the story that 'one dies', an interminable story since it cannot be defined in relation to a personal, authentic being-there-towards-death.[23] Malone does not recount his own death, but his *not*

---

20 *Henosis* is the term used in Platonist and neo-Platonist philosophy to designate the mystical unification with the One. [Trans.]

21 See E. M. Cioran's 'Beckett' in *Anathemas and Admirations* (Richard Howard trans.) (New York: Arcade Publishing, 2012), p. 136. This is a fundamental text for the explanation of the term 'lessness', to which we shall return extensively.

22 Samuel Beckett, *Ill Seen Ill Said* in *Nohow On*, pp. 81–82.

knowing if he will die, or, rather, his not ceasing to croak. And this is not even his *own* doubt, so much as the *exhausted* breath that comes to us from a *cosmic* place: the world appears there, I throw open the window and it appears to me, but 'He'd snatch away his hand and go back into his corner. Appalled. All he had seen was ashes'.[24] How would one not think that 'this has gone on long enough?'

> CLOV: Yes! (*Pause.*) What?
>
> HAMM: This . . . this . . . thing.
>
> [. . .]
>
> HAMM: You stink already. The whole place stinks of corpses.
>
> CLOV: The whole universe.[25]

And yet it lasts. It is a day like the others. The inability to represent death; the impossibility of freeing us from the 'impression we exist': 'We always find something, eh Didi, to give us the impression we exist?'[26] 'Not to be' is impossible: 'We'll hang ourselves tomorrow'.[27] In the meantime, something nevertheless happens: 'It's never the same pus from one second to the next.' Moreover, they 'have to talk about it'.[28]

What acting, what *drama* corresponds to the 'impression of existing'? 'Nothing to be done' are its first words. From the representation of action par excellence, the *drama* has become expression of being always and only 'potentially'. Up to relinquishing even of this 'waiting' for the 'act'. Vladimir is the *persona* of the first

---

23 See the important book-length essay by Nadia Fusini, *B&B. Beckett & Bacon* (Milan: Garzanti, 1994).

24 Samuel Beckett, *Endgame* in *Complete Dramatic Works* (London: Faber and Faber, 1986), p. 113.

25 Beckett, *Endgame*, p. 114.

26 Samuel Beckett, *Waiting for Godot* in *Complete Dramatic Works*, p. 64.

27 Beckett, *Waiting for Godot*, p. 88.

28 Beckett, *Waiting for Godot*, pp. 56 and 58.

moment of this metamorphosis. '[S]aying, Vladimir, be reasonable, you haven't yet tried everything. And I resumed the struggle.'[29] Struggle is a keyword for K., as we saw. Vladimir shows he has not forgotten it, when he seeks to shake, to 'reawaken' Estragon. And Estragon's ever-looming sleep is the same as K.'s in his 'last night'. A sleep that awaits without proceeding, a waiting that is no longer *at-tending*. K.'s impatience, Hamlet's reluctant tarrying have now reached their end 'game'. Patience is only a powerlessness to act; the time of tarrying no longer prepares anything. Vladimir and Estragon's waiting-without-waiting, which might have represented the only true 'end' of *The Castle*, is the absolutely 'imperfect' conclusion of K.'s impatience. Nor would the tarrying have been able to 'save' Hamlet, who remains a tragic hero destined to action, to the *drân* despite everything. K. empties his impotence to the point of impotent waiting; Hamlet acts, and acts 'effectively', but only to recognize in the end that he does not recognize himself, does not express his own daemon-character. Hamlet would like to 'withdraw' from acting, to live without having to await anything, and hence to die perfectly. K. leads action to the point where all that remains is the ruin of waiting, the waiting for Godot, unmoving, fixed in a 'desire' that is therefore inexhaustible.

For the tragic hero, the 'context,' the confrontation with the *ethos*, is necessary. The conciliation between the character of the hero and the common *ethos*, the *xynón* [common], already becomes problematic in classical tragedy, but it is assumed as a *theme* in modern drama, in the *Trauerspiel*: the mourning scene as the undecidability of conciliation. No *drân* can ground it. The 'hero' can only avail himself of the paradoxical *ethos* of the search, of the interrogation—in

---

29 Beckett, *Waiting for Godot*, p. 11.

principle, as *ethos without site*. Nevertheless, Hamlet has before him a 'community', despite its values appearing confused and in crisis, not only in his eyes but also in those of his antagonists, such as Claudius and the Queen. And K. would like to 'enter' into a 'community', however incomprehensible to him seems the *ethos* that supports it. With Beckett, however, every epic-tragic meridian is inexorably *past*. Community and history are absent. The theme of relations is contracted to its minimal dimension, reduced to a fine line:[30] to the *two*. Since *on parle, man spricht*, 'it is said', to be two is inevitable—and it is inevitable that, in ek-sisting, these two have alongside them those 'responsible' for their birth; it is necessary that from the depths of the past (the dustbins) emerge the progenitors ('Scoundrel! Why did you engender me?').[31] But if the other exists as a nightmare, *against* me, 'how can I be?'; if the face of the other no longer reflects me, is no longer the 'place' where I can *reflect* myself

---

30 In *The World as Will and Representation*, Schopenhauer describes Shakespeare's writing as a line that gradually grows, dilates, thickens. It is the opposite operation to that of Beckett—and of Giacometti's sculpture. How often did Giacometti trace, wittingly or not, Beckett's face? A physiognomic consideration would force us to study the 'masks' of Beckett, Wittgenstein, Giacometti, and Buster Keaton. ['Shakespearian tragedy . . . is like a line that has width as well: it leaves itself time, it expatiates: there are speeches and even entire scenes that do not advance the action or even really concern it, but in which we nevertheless get to know more about the acting characters or their situations, and this lets us understand even the action more thoroughly. The action remains the focus, but not so exclusively that we forget in the last instance its intention is to portray the human essence and existence in general.' Arthur Schopenhauer, *The World as Will and Representation*, VOL. 2 (Judith Norman, Alistair Welchman and Christopher Janaway trans and eds) (Cambridge: Cambridge University Press, 2018), p. 453. —Trans.]

31 Beckett, *Endgame*, p. 116.

but, contrastingly, has become enigmatic, the I itself will become nothing but the 'place' of its own going astray. 'Yes I remember. That was I. That was I then.'[32] The I *was*. Now nothing remains but the voice that reaches 'to one'[33] in the dark, this 'hearer'[34] perhaps entirely inert as far as 'mental activity'[35] goes and 'that cankerous other'[36] who still presumes he can describe such 'company'. But the 'fable' is already, ultimately, 'the fable of one with you in the dark. The fable of one fabling of one with you in the dark.'[37] The fable of the I, 'unnameable', 'unthinkable', '[n]owhere to be sought'.[38] Give up on it, drop it.

Do the two, chained to each other in an irrepressible 'conversation',[39] reveal the purgatorial aspect of the work that Beckett recognized in his teacher Joyce? The reference to Dante's Belacqua has long been a recognized *topos* in the critical literature. (This is a *topos* that Beckett himself imposes. Just think of the explicit reference to the episode and posture of Dante's character in

---

32 Beckett, *Company* in *Nohow On*, p. 17.

33 Beckett, *Company*, p. 5.

34 Beckett, *Company*, p. 20.

35 Beckett, *Company*, p. 7.

36 Beckett, *Company*, p. 6.

37 Beckett, *Company*, pp. 51–52.

38 Beckett, *Company*, p. 19.

39 Peter Szondi, *Theory of Modern Drama* (Michael Hays trans.) (Minneapolis, MN: University of Minnesota Press, 1987), p. 8. But it is the entirety of Szondi's contributions to the history of modern drama that remain irreplaceable even for the understanding of Beckett's 'break'. Beckett, after Artaud and Jarry, understood that European theatre 'exhausts' itself in conversation; it becomes a theatre of 'words', betraying its own *drân*. Theatre-drama is the *body* of the word. Its 'exhaustion' in interminable, immobile conversation has been demonstrated in all its tragic comicality by the early Ionesco.

Company: 'Thus you now on our back in the dark once sat huddled there your body having shown it could go out no more').[40] Dante the pilgrim comes to a stop before the figure who sits clasping his knees 'holding his face down low between them'.[41] Will he be 'vigorous'[42] enough to climb the hill, to enter the 'castle'? And will he too be 'obliged'[43] to sit? Will not even Dante be tempted to ask, 'Oh brother, what good would climbing do?'[44] This is Estragon's refrain: there is nothing to be done. But none of love's negligence is 'restored'[45] in *Waiting for Godot*, that 'slack love'[46]—'unpregnant'[47] as Hamlet will say, not 'pregnant' with his cause, his duty. The condition is thus not at all 'purgatorial'. But not even the colour of *akedia*, of sloth, dominates the conversation. The latter is in fact *infernal*. It is an aspect of the unhappy ire in the face of the 'sweet air', which 'envies' all 'that the sun makes glad'.[48] Of this 'we were'[49] we can certainly find clearer traces in Beckett than in Belacqua's disenchanted, but

---

40 Beckett, *Company*, p. 50.

41 Dante Alighieri, *The Divine Comedy of Dante, Volume 2: Purgatorio* (Robert M. Durling trans. and ed.) (Oxford: Oxford University Press, 2003), Canto 4, line 108, p. 69. My impression is that Beckett is particularly struck by Belacqua's *posture*. On this, see p. 91n63 in this volume.

42 Dante, *Purgatorio*, Canto 4, line 114, p. 71.

43 Dante, *Purgatorio*, Canto 4, line 98, p. 69.

44 Dante, *Purgatorio*, Canto 4, line 127, p. 71.

45 Dante, *Purgatorio*, Canto 17, line 86, p. 281.

46 Dante, *Purgatorio*, Canto 17, line 130, p. 283.

47 Shakespeare, *Hamlet* 2.2.1642.

48 Dante Alighieri, *The Divine Comedy of Dante, Volume 1: Inferno* (Robert M. Durling trans. and ed.) (Oxford: Oxford University Press, 1996), Canto 7, line 122, p. 119.

49 Dante, *Inferno*, Canto 7, line 123, p. 119.

se-cure,[50] waiting; and yet envy (not wanting to see, wanting for the other not to be, in order not to have to see him), just like repentance ('And if we repented? ESTRAGON: Repented what? [. . .] Our being born?'),[51] belongs to being-there understood as inter-est, *Mit-sein,* and can thus only bring to life epic-dramatic plots.[52] To Beckett's *personae* little is left but the 'care' for the illusion of existing or of not being nothing.[53] They cannot be placed in a space that is either infernal or purgatorial. Their condition is exclusively *a-oikos,* 'homeless', but not in the sense of being-suspended nor in that of proceeding *en route* [*per via*]. They are immobile *on* the route, as though 'rooted' in it. They do not even find themselves *in* a landscape:

HAMM: Nature has forgotten us.

---

50 Cacciari writes *se-cura* instead of *sicura,* to make explicit the etymological link between security / secure (*sicurezza / sicura*) and the care of the self (*la cura di sé*). [Trans.]

51 Beckett, *Waiting for Godot,* p. 13.

52 Cacciari's neologism, *inter-esse* associates togetherness, interrelation, *inter* with 'being', the root of *essere,* 'being', 'to be'. *Interesse* also means 'interest'. This is relatively straightforward to render in English as I have with 'inter-est', where again 'inter' is a relational prefix whereas *est* comes from the French 'to be', drawing on the Anglo-French Norman—ultimately Latin-rooted—*interesse.* The Heideggerian *Mit-sein,* referenced here, is rendered in English translations as 'being-with'. [Trans.]

53 Here we encounter the most clearly Leopardian aspect of Beckett, as Aldo Tagliaferri and others have underlined (see the 'Introduzione' to Samuel Beckett, *Trilogia* [Aldo Tagliaferri trans. and ed.] [Turin: Einaudi, 1996]). Tagliaferri's reference to Severino's interpretation of Leopardi is correct (Emanuele Severino, *Il nulla e la poesia* [Milan: Rizzoli, 1990]). And one arrives again at Kafka: '*Can* you know anything other than deception? If ever the deception is annihilated, you must not look in that direction or you will turn into a pillar of salt'. 'Reflections on Sin, Suffering, Hope, and the True Way', in *Wedding Preparations in the Country,* p. 52.

CLOV: There's no more nature.[54]

The decline of the 'Nomos of the Earth' constitutes *Hamlet*'s prophecy.[55] And if the landscape of the Schloss appears entirely 'earthly', its Nomos now seems 'illegible' to the interrogating I, who has become a stranger to himself. In Beckett, the 'earth' becomes confused with the immobility of the 'two'; even the memory that from it a *ius* [law] could arise has become lost. Everything has happened— and the cause of this happening is unnameable. But the ignorance of the cause renders everything unnameable. Yet affirming that nothing remains to be done does not silence the problem, because precisely this continues to be said—and this coercion to say, to repeat, testifies to the powerlessness to die. Speaking of it and writing of it, we become complicit with this impotence. This is the complicity of literature, in spite of it all—and, at the same time, its responsibility: only in this way does it correspond to the fact that, even after the last day, 'one lives'. The I that 'one lives' is empty, another wreck left behind by the tidal wave, and yet one of its signs—a real sign and, at the same time, *sinnlos*, without a comprehensible meaning. Sign without 'destiny', and yet heir to that power that named, judged, accused. A terribly unhappy heir, as all heirs are destined to be after Hamlet; forced to extend the search for meaning (which implies its absence) through the *ingens sylva*[56] of interpretations, without being able to believe that a Book, a Nomos constitutes meaning's origin and

---

54 Beckett, *Endgame*, p. 97.

55 I have translated *tramonto*, which also means 'twilight', as 'decline' to gesture towards Oswald Spengler, author of *The Decline of the West* (1918), who alongside Carl Schmitt, author of *The Nomos of the Earth* (1950), is a pivotal figure in the German Conservative Revolution and is quite possibly alluded to here. [Trans.]

56 Latin expression meaning mighty, vast or immense forest, for instance in Virgil, *Aeneid* 7.676–77. [Trans.]

foundation. An heir 'contracted' to the most naked, the poorest of images, oscillating between unnameable desire and the impossible 'nobility' of silence.

Hamlet would like to remain alone but cannot. K. remains alone but does not want to be. The movements conjoin in Beckett: the 'couples' of his theatre are in perfect despair about being able to ever attain authentic solitude. And it is inevitably so: indeed, even solitude exists in a social dimension, like that 'energy' which contests its presupposition: that man is a *zoon politikón*. In solitude, one is never truly alone but always in polemical relation with that assumption. Like Prospero having retreated to the island, where his activity [*fare*] even reaches the summit of power by becoming *magic*. It is in solitude that the mind can reach the peak of concentration, that the Cogito truly expresses itself as the Centre of a circumference whose radius is infinite. Beckett's 'solitaries' have instead completely lost the way that leads to the power of solitude. When they 'think', they but 'realize' the *comic* reversal of that Cogito. This is what happens when it is Lucky who 'puts his mind to thinking', or when in the course of Act II, Vladimir breaks with the tone of the 'conversation' in 'noble' sounding asides: 'Let us not waste our time in idle discourse! [Pause. Vehemently.] Let us do something, while we have the chance!';[57] 'Was I sleeping, while others suffered?'[58] Solitude never 'produces' anything but the *recitation* of thought. The doing of the Cogito is completely reduced to Lucky and Vladimir's 'to act'.

Because all the protagonists of Beckett's theatre perform a role, recitation and life coincide. Here too the 'Hamletic perspective' reaches its epilogue. In some of Beckett's characters, like Pozzo, the

---

57 Beckett, *Waiting for Godot*, p. 74.
58 Beckett, *Waiting for Godot*, p. 84.

identity of the two dimensions is 'programmatic' ('A little attention,
if you please. [. . .] But be a little more attentive, for pity's sake. [. . .]
How did you find me? [VLADIMIR *and* ESTRAGON *look at him blankly.*]
Good? Fair? Middling? Poor? Positively badly?').[59] Their very names
clearly reveal their 'theatrical vocation'; but it is a lapsed 'vocation'.
They represent the leftovers of the 'to act': clowns, mummers,
unravelled masks; at the same time, precisely this 'to act' must attain
the 'cruelty' of the language of the body, of the injured body, it must
for this 'theatre' 'abandon' the dominion of the word. (Artaud had
'exposed' himself to such a consequence well before Beckett.)

The arrival of Pozzo with his 'slave' Lucky is revelatory of this
situation. He seems to impersonate energy and decision-making compared to the two who are waiting, but at the moment of leaving he
puts on an exhilarating pantomime on the not *de-ciding-for-oneself*[60]
from that place where he has ended up (such a pantomime explains
its sense in *Ill Seen Ill Said*: 'She still without stopping. On her way
without starting. Gone without going. Back without returning').[61] His
return in Act II, blind and seeking help, reiterates with the highest
cosmic *violence* the *fiction* of power, the fact that power is by now
nothing but representation, 'to act'. The illusion of existing cannot
express itself other than by *in-luding*.[62] But it will not be discourses
that can 'order' the *game*; its language will have to 'erase itself' to the
point of becoming transformed into sound, curse, gesture, act without

---

59 Beckett, *Waiting for Godot*, pp. 36–37.

60 In hyphenating *de-cidersi*, Cacciari is again emphasizing the etymology
of the word 'decide' (see p. 18n29 in this volume). *Decidersi* is reflexive,
hence the rather cumbersome formulation given here: 'de-ciding-for-oneself'.
[Trans.]

61 Beckett, *Ill Seen Ill Said* in *Nohow On*, p. 66.

62 This neologism, *in-ludendo*, appears to bring together the Latin *ludens*,
'playing', and the Italian *illudere*, 'to delude', to subject 'to illusion'. [Trans.]

words.[63] It will thus be possible to show what is unnameable. Beckett 'adopts' the same *facies* as Wittgenstein. But here the mystical, *das Mystische*, ultimately shows itself in the mute rhythm of the 'comic'.

This rhythm is that of total immanence. The figure denuded of all 'ulteriority'; figures reciprocally chained to their very conversing, nailed to their path—these are comical in their essence. It is the comic which 'says the truth': that the dialogue has 'fallen' to *sinnlos* conversation; that nothing remains to be done but to feign doing; that the different *personae*, even the most dissimilar, such as master and servant, are ultimately in-different. It is the comic which tears down all pretence of still being able to make the Word 'proceed', of avoiding its being silenced. It is its *impotence* which forces words to the essential economy of the gesture, of being *always less*. Once again it is the clown, the 'fool' who has the last word—but the last word is *sans*, without itself, without object, verb or predicate; it ignores the accusative. It corresponds to 'Lessness'—and not to *Losigkeit*, as the term is translated into German by Beckett himself; Lessness has nothing to do with dissolving, with solution, with the possibility of separating-from oneself, de-ciding oneself. Lessness is the *loss* of all this. We had begun to grasp this in Kafka's prose; Beckett 'realizes' it in its insuperable form. But how can Lessness be said to be 'completed'? Once again, a comic paradox.

---

63 See Gilles Deleuze, 'The Exhausted' in *Essays Critical and Clinical* (Michael A. Greco and Daniel W. Smith trans) (Minneapolis, MN: University of Minnesota Press, 1997). This is an essential essay for the study of Beckett, interpreted from the standpoint of a 'relentless Spinozism' (p. 152). There is no longer any 'possible'. And nothing remains but to continue to finish. It will, however, be necessary to link these considerations—as we shall do subsequently—with the Kojèvian reading of Hegel. It is the very exhaustiveness of the concept, the exhaustion of the concept itself, that Beckett demonstrates as exhausted. It is Discourse that is no longer 'possible'—and yet that persists in being-exhausted.

Lessness: the image of being-there imploding into pure immanence.

BOY: What am I to say to Mr Godot, sir?

VLADIMIR: Tell him . . . (*he hesitates*) . . . tell him you saw us. (*Pause.*) You did see us, didn't you?[64]

In pure immanence, semblance and being coincide like immobility and becoming. Apparently, the situations mutate, time has not stopped ('VLADIMIR: Time has stopped. POZZO: [*Cuddling his watch to his ear.*] Don't you believe it, sir, don't you believe it'),[65] but it is precisely a case of clock time; the *who* of time is missing. Missing this essential dimension, time marks only the appearance of different events, prisoners of the stage itself. Mere Chronos, which causes nothing to be out of joint, bringing with it no *novitas*. This is the time of the Schloss. Everything is repeated, without being the same; everything changes, without ever being able to indicate why.

> Have you not done tormenting me with your accursed time! It's abominable! When! When! One day, is that not enough for you, one day like any other day, one day he went dumb, one day I went blind, one day we'll go deaf, one day we were born, one day we shall die, the same day, the same second, is that not enough for you?.[66]

And in *Endgame*:

HAMM: [. . .] What time is it?

CLOV: The same as usual.

HAMM: [. . .] Have you looked?

CLOV: Yes.

---

64 Beckett, *Waiting for Godot*, p. 50.

65 Beckett, *Waiting for Godot*, p. 36.

66 Beckett, *Waiting for Godot*, p. 83.

HAMM: Well?

CLOV: Zero.[67]

The time is the same in which the opposites take place, seeing and not seeing, being born and dying, because they return eternally while remaining as they are in their real opposition. No hour retains memories of past metamorphoses and no hour attends the gods to-come. Untranscendendable *facts* are represented in time. The world is comprehended, summarized and *exhausted* in them.

'What age is at?'[68] Perhaps the age of time 'devoured' by the concept? 'CLOSED PLACE. All needed to be known for say is known'.[69] Is this the idea aimed at by the *mise-en-scène*? Was Beckett informed of the 'epochal' *Lectures* held by Kojève on the *Phenomenology* to the '*maîtres à penser*' of 1930s Paris, still the capital of Europe? 'Hegel was able to close the History of Philosophy (and hence History in general) and inaugurate the age of Wisdom . . . by *identifying* the Concept with Time'; such an identity '"reveals" itself as uni-total or "circular" *Discourse* (Logos), namely, as an ensemble—coherent and *one* in itself—of *all* the discourses that constitute the human content of universal History, *en ensemble* which is the real and *integral* presence of the Spirit in the World.'[70] Beckett is the perfect negative of this philosophy of history with no more history. No action can alter its concept. Every apparent transformation is pre-determined, prejudged by it, nothing but an occurrence within the already unfolded presence of the Spirit of the World. The totality of facts unfolds

---

67 Beckett, *Endgame*, p. 94.

68 James Joyce, *Finnegans Wake* (Oxford: Oxford University Press, 2012), p. 213.

69 Beckett, 'Fizzles V' in *The Complete Short Prose: 1929–1989* (S. E. Gontarski ed.) (New York: Grove Press, 1995), p. 236.

70 Alexandre Kojève, 'Le concept et le temps', *Deucalion* 5 (1955): 18–19.

entirely under the gaze of *theoria*; every fact is *destined* to be. History and destiny coincide in the term *Geschichte*. Everything appears complete and yet everything is still underway. Everything in the concept is given simultaneously. Beckett will say '*La soudaineté de tout*! The suddenness of all'.[71] Is this not the 'content' of his entire oeuvre?

But the representation of this content, its performance overturns its meaning. After the last day, when nothing decisive is left to be done, that is, when no thought can fully realize itself in action and no discourse can comprehend it, it is not the concept that instals itself as master over the tragedy of becoming, enabling us victoriously to bear contradiction. Rather, it is the weariness of spirit that is incapable even of feigning its own movement. Belacqua's 'antechamber' has become a permanent station. Even the 'we were' of sad slothfulness, the envious and dull struggle against life has disappeared here or reappears only in bursts, since the two—Vladimir–Estragon, Hamm–Clov—display the intolerable torment at being unable to be entirely alone. There is no longer an argument for continuing. Faith was the evidence of things unseen.[72] Is it only through faith that one could continue the apparent life, incapable of dying? Is this faith in Godot? It cannot be, if not as its 'comic' reversal, since faith, each faith, is at-tendence, *pistis eis*,[73] while here the only 'run up' is Pozzo's.

---

71 Beckett, *Ill Seen Ill Said* in *Nohow On*, p. 66. [Cacciari places the original French alongside the Italian translation, as I have here with the English. —Trans.]

72 Cacciari is drawing on Hebrews 11:1 and its vision of faith as the 'substance of things hoped for, the evidence of things unseen', in Italian: *sostanza di cose sperate e argomento di cose non viste*. [Trans.]

73 *Pistis* in Classical Greek was an expression for 'trust' or 'belief', later assuming the more Christian sense of 'faith'; whereas *eis* means 'in', 'unto', 'towards'. So 'faith in' is the most literal translation of *pistis eis*. The debates on the different ways of rendering *pistis eis*, particularly in *Romans*, have had considerable implications for soteriology going back to Luther. [Trans.]

The 'leap' towards the unforeseeable *Adveniens* would be conceivable only by 'arriving at' [*adendo*][74] the radical critique of Hegelian Sophia. This was Kierkegaard's path, which Kafka loved as 'impossible', and which is also exhausted in Beckett. That last Discourse, that of Hegel, left only these presences, these 'derailed' bodies. That discourse has by now so 'much' taken place as to appear forgotten in those bodies, to survive as if it were the forgotten past of their obsessive, interminable 'conversation'.

This outcome 'surpasses' the dialectical system precisely because it is produced by its completion, just like the completion of the *epos* in *Ulysses*. It is the 'fullness' of both forms that generates the Lessness. What remains to be written after Joyce? What is there to be *systematically* thought after Hegel? What is to be written or to be thought once the history of the world is 'accomplished' in the concept? Nothing but a mere exposition of events, which occur in a time whose destination it remains impossible to say, a zero-time. Is this not the other, inevitable, aspect of the Hegelian synthesis and of Joyce's 'masterpiece'? Becket *unveils* it. History as the history of Knowledge is destined to be accomplished, and to end up *without use*. The timbre of the *consummatum est* rings out at the heights of Sophia itself. And it is the echo of that timbre that 'falls' in Estragon's immobility, in the anonymous 'you-he' who in *Company* lies on its back in the dark. The 'fever' of the concept, the 'furious restlessness' of all great Form must end; they cannot but arrive at the point of their exhaustion. Must the rose blossom in the cross of the present?[75]

---

74 Cacciari is playing with the fact that the verb *adire* contains *ire*, 'becoming'. [Trans.]

75 The reference is to G. W. F. Hegel, *Elements of the Philosophy of Right* (H. B. Nisbet trans., Allen W. Wood ed.) (Cambridge: Cambridge University Press, 1991), p. 22: 'To recognise reason as the rose in the cross of the present'. [Trans.]

Yes—but the rose must wilt. This is what Beckett knows 'beyond' Hegel.[76] Anything but 'irrationalism'. For Hegel the End is the thought-of-thought, thought satisfied with itself, eternally proximate to itself in the fullness of its contents. For Beckett, this same fullness represents the contraction of thought onto bare being-there. Hegel's fullness becomes absolute loss of all ek-static power. No path, not even K.'s imperfect ones, can depart from here.

Can we imagine a secret 'teacher' from whom Beckett learnt this extraordinary reception-overturning of Hegel's lesson? We have already encountered him: it is one of his Italians, Vico. The power of reflection quite naturally moves to the 'point' where it finds self-satisfaction and hence is united with the 'infinite knowledge of God'[77] (and does not merely desire to be, as Vico concludes in his *Scienza*). This is the peace that it yearns for. But this is precisely the peace that consumes all contradiction within itself, since it fails to conceive of being as anything other than the product of thought, and so treats it as nothing in itself. The most radical 'scepticism' with respect to the *thing-in-itself* is thus always accompanied by the 'haughtiness' of the Cogito. But once reflection reaches its final meridian, it turns into the daemon-character of a new *barbarism*. Indeed, reason satisfied with itself demands that every individual, which it comprehends in the concept, be satisfied. It demands that every 'passion' be *justified*, since

---

76 The fundamental error of Lukács critique, against which Adorno battles not without some uncertainty, consists precisely in not understanding how Beckett's 'nihilism' represents the opposite of a re-actionary movement with respect to the Hegelian dialectic. Instead, he 'pays for' the realization of the dialectic in Sophia. It is the 'victorious' Sophia that 'saves' the phenomenon by annihilating it, which is to say, transforming it into *nothing* other than its *positum*.

77 Giambattista Vico, *New Science* (Dave Marsh trans.) (Harmondsworth: Penguin, 1999), p. 491.

nothing irrational is given if time has resolved itself in the concept. It demands that every *objectum* is nothing but the *positum* of the freedom of the subject, at its complete disposal. The heterogenesis of ends: the completion of reflection becomes the unravelling of community, of every community; whether it be the community between individual and individual on the basis of a 'common' that, as such, belongs to no one, or the community of all individuals with the original sense of the *physis*.

> HAMM: The waves, how are the waves?
>
> CLOV: The waves? (*He turns the telescope on the waves.*) Lead.
>
> HAMM: And the sun?
>
> CLOV: (*Looking.*) Zero.[78]

The triumph of Sophia cannot presume to affirm itself as the Last, the Ultimate. Vico demonstrates this according to the design of his 'providential' history; Leopardi, by explaining the nexus of reason-nihilism; whereas Beckett does so through the further passage from the forgetting of 'realized metaphysics' to the return of the 'barbarism of the senses'.[79] 'Malice of reflection' (Vico)[80] ultimately affirms the identity of 'accomplished sense' and the absence of further sense, between fullness and Lessness. 'Full' time leaves an unbridgeable emptiness.

> VLADIMIR: And where were we yesterday evening according to you?
>
> ESTRAGON: How do I know? In another compartment. There's no lack of void.[81]

---

78 Beckett, *Endgame*, p. 107.

79 On the 'barbarism of the senses', see Vico, *New Science*, p. 488.

80 Vico, *New Science*, p. 488.

81 Beckett, *Waiting for Godot*, p. 61.

For Vico, this new 'barbarism of the senses', its appeal, can represent the 'primitive simplicity of the early world of peoples'.[82] A 'forecast' that is unfounded and unfoundable, even in light of *The New Science* itself. Leopardi and Beckett ruthlessly disenchant Vico's hope, revealing its most authentic and dramatic foundation. Culture must generate Terror, and Terror, the desert. No pilgrim can go *to* the desert any longer, nor does any voice come *from* the desert. The fundamental historical 'types' are included on this meridian: the master–servant dialectic between Pozzo and Lucky is locked in on itself, lacking all 'progressive' energy (analogous, perhaps, to the village-Schloss?); the impotence, still 'comically' reminiscent of Vladimir's hope-principle; the image of Belacqua, of the nostalgia of being-there to 'free itself' from inter-est, reduced to mere negligence in Estragon; the 'imperfect' and impotent solitude of Hamm and Clov, immobile in their 'run-up' to go—all figures for feeling incapable of unfolding in *percipere* and from there, and beyond, in *comprehension*. The itinerary, the great *Bildungsroman* of the *Phenomenology*, recurs at its start. But it is a recurrence [*ricorso*][83] that is not a prelude to anything else.

Wreckage of the *Phenomenology*, wreckage of the history that should have concluded in a *theosophy*. In the new 'barbarism of the senses', the knowledge-*gnosis* of God-in-history becomes the stuttering or unnameable demand that expresses itself in glances, gestures, pantomimes that no *Discourse* could ever 'translate'. Discourse is Will to order, *command*: that every entity assumes its proper place in the inflexible form of the System; that every entity re-place and overcome itself. Clov, who picks up the objects scattered on the ground *mimes the Aufhebung*!

---

82 Vico, *New Science*, p. 489.

83 Vico's theory of history as a cycle of repetitions is encapsulated in the formula *corsi e ricorsi*. [Trans.]

HAMM: [. . .] What are you doing?

CLOV: Putting things in order. (*He straightens up. Fervently.*) I'm going to clear everything away! (*He starts picking up again.*)

HAMM: Order!

CLOV: (*Straightening up.*) I love order. It's my dream. A world where all would be silent and still and each thing in its last place, under the last dust.[84]

It is in dialogues such as these that Beckett reveals himself to be the 'heir' to the ultimate meaning of idealism. The dream of Order, of idealism's Reason, can develop logically only in the direction of the desert, of the 'last dust'. The apparently 'elementary' life of Beckett's characters, upto the near vegetative state of Nell and Nagg, does not represent the opposite of Culture, but precisely the leftovers that conclude its history, the product of its 'digestion'. They are prisoners of Historical knowledge as binned rubbish, indicating the 'bestial brutum' *at the end* of metaphysics, in no way the first unconscious cries for the 'salvation' it promised.

However, 'concluding' in the *pax profonda* of that dust remains a dream. That everything goes silent is a dream. Wrecks or ruins of the world *exist*, traces of what once was faith, waiting, searching, action and non-action, illusion, disillusionment. *Insecuritas* continues to want to say itself, despite not harbouring even the idea of being able to 'overcome' itself. It is the condition of the Ulysses of literature and philosophy, under the sign of Hamlet, of K., of Stephen Dedalus. Beckett 'reveals' its last name: No one.[85] Only this name 'fits'

---

84 Beckett, *Endgame*, p. 120.

85 'No one moulds us again out of earth and clay, / No one conjures our dust. No one.' Paul Celan, 'Psalm' in *Selected Poems* (Michael Hamburger and Christopher Middleton trans) (Harmondsworth: Penguin, 1995), p. 179.

Lessness; only those *without* a name can signal towards the anonymous 'barbarism' of in-difference, the dust that blankets everything. K. conserves a trace of his almost extinguished origin;[86] in the 'endgame', he forgets his very name. He is announced by both Barnabas and the Boy of *Waiting for Godot*, who have nothing to announce; no Annunciation for No one. The novel could go on infinitely; Vladimir and Estragon repeat 'shall we go?' to the point

---

Not only Celan as an indefatigable reader of Kafka, but Celan *with* Beckett. And yet, even when delving into the 'Black and infinite' (Beckett's 'grey'), into the 'never again', the elegiac timbre the *Klagendelied*, never fades from the *Klagendelied*, which remains absent or is even ruthlessly parodied by Beckett.

86 When K. calls at the Schloss, he presents himself with a 'sudden decision' (Kafka, *Castle*, p. 21) as 'the land surveyor's assistant'. 'What assistant?' asks a 'harsh, arrogant voice' at the end. ' "Joseph" said K.' But were his assistants not called Arthur and Jeremiah? Insists the voice, showing itself to be well-informed. No, they are the new ones replies K. 'No, those are the old ones' repeats the Schloss. But K.: ' "I'm the old one, I rejoined the land surveyor today." "No," the voice now shouted. "Who am I then?" K. asked.' After a brief pause, the same voice, even if 'it was like another, deeper voice, one commanding greater respect' replies in a completely unexpected way: 'You're the old assistant' (p. 22). What does this episode mean? Why, after a brief pause, do they accept K.'s version, which they had only just rejected, at the Schloss? Is it 'good' for the Schloss that K. is Joseph? Is his identity, like his profession, unimportant? No one chases them away; they can fight with whatever name they wish. Which in any case does not *count*, is worthless. Or instead, does Joseph K. really return? Among K.'s few memories, none seems to have anything to do with Joseph's story. And yet the latter must 'follow him'. Joseph is clearly called, *called to account*. No one accuses K. and his very 'call' is dubious. Does he wish to be 'called'? This will 'follows' the 'case' that strikes Joseph. Joseph dies 'badly', like a dog. Instead, K. could even survive indefinitely. This 'possibility' must 'follow' the end of Joseph. K. is, I would say, Joseph *sub specie aeternitatis*, 'purified' of all that which, in the preceding novel, might have been accidental, indefinite or simply 'absurd'.

of the impossible exhaustion of Lessness itself. The border is reached—and the border is nowhere; and so it cannot be transgressed. One does not 'overcome' it other than by in-sisting upon it, immobile like that tree that is the play's only landscape:

POZZO: What is it like?

VLADIMIR: (*Looking round.*) It's indescribable. It's like nothing. There's nothing. There's a tree.'[87]

The land surveyor's question is blocked *en route*, becoming transformed into the waiting *of No one*, in all the senses of the genitive. The desire to access the Other manifests itself in all its aporetic character and transforms itself in a paradoxical desire-for-nothing (not even to *nullify* itself, which would in any case imply the idea of doing, of a 'decisive' action). In waiting without time, without community, without landscape, No one manifests the nothing as the essence of its being-there and 'allows' the full disenchantment of its illusions to take place—of illusion *par excellence*, above all that which we have continually encountered: to be able to *perficere*[88] life in real death, 'happy' in itself. Instead, the nothing of being-there must continue to reveal itself, to appear; were it not to, it would be unable to constitute 'truth'. Kojève had repeated to his French 'students': to appear is essential to essence.

What does '*on attend*'?[89] What do the No ones await? The equivalent of their names, the god in their image: Clov-Clown, Pierrot-Godot. The 'etymon' has no importance; the 'meaning' is irrelevant. It is the *sound* that decides. The 'first' image, the *Arché* that founded and destined the End, 'saving' the phenomena, became a sound that

---

87 Beckett, *Waiting for Godot*, p. 81.
88 In Latin, 'to bring to an end', 'to finish, conclude'. [Trans.]
89 'One waits'. Cacciari cites the original French. [Trans.]

irresistibly harks back not to Doing, but to the poorest 'to act'. The highest Entity is 'thrown' into it: Godot, God-*out*, 'out' of itself, irrevocably expelled from its own *absoluta potentia*. He has lost his real name forever; like Estragon and Vladimir, he too is left only with a clown's name. The Invisible, towards which hope directed itself—firmly believing in it as it did so—is the name-sound, not even an object lost in the undertow. Was it thus from the start? Or did it end up like this due to our negligence, to fatigue of the heart and mind, to the indolence of the 'we were', because we could not be strong enough to bear the weight of the Invisible, to remain 'responsible' towards the Unnameable, because that *command* was: 'thou shalt not make unto thee images' too 'sublime' for us? We cannot know. The *fact* is this, 'closed' in immanence: Godot will each day return to not coming. And even if he did, he would be Godot, and no Godot can ever 'save'. But was this not the 'truth' that his supreme Names hid?

Desperatio de salute—since what 'salvation' now means is incomprehensible. One awaits as if a saviour were due, but not knowing what he would achieve.

> VLADIMIR: Two thieves, crucified at the same time as our Saviour. One—
>
> ESTRAGON: Our what?
>
> VLADIMIR: Our Saviour. Two thieves. One is supposed to have been saved and the other . . . (*he searches for the contrary of saved*) . . . damned.
>
> ESTRAGON: Saved from what?[90]

The tidal wave has upset the hope and faith in the Invisible. One waits; the wait has become entirely separated from hope, becoming identified with the illusion of existing and inevitability of surviving.

---

90 Beckett, *Waiting for Godot*, p. 14.

One waits to cease waiting, to extinguish waiting. For it is because of the waiting that we 'stir', but we do so while immobilized in our wait (*Stirrings Still*).[91] It is because of the waiting that the 'gropings of the mind' ceaselessly repeat themselves.[92] Godot is tomorrow's emptiness, the image of an 'eternal return' in perfect despair about the *power* to impress its seal on being. A 'comical' reversal of Nietzsche, as previously of Hegel. Godot continues not to come, like the 'two' do not *go*, do not die. Just as waiting for the 'two' is not at-tending, not acting, in the same way Godot does not come because he does nothing, whereas to reveal himself would be the doing *par excellence*.

> VLADIMIR: What does he do, Mr Godot? (*Silence.*) Do you hear me?
>
> BOY: Yes, sir.
>
> VLADIMIR: Well?
>
> BOY: He does nothing, sir. (*Silence.*)[93]

However, Godot is not *incuriosus*. The Boy had asked Vladimir what he should tell him. Well? Is there a hint to a 'time' when perhaps Godot would have 'done' something? Is there reflected in Godot the idea of the exhausted *poietés*, as in the literature after Joyce or, as Kojève would have said, in painting after the *absolute* work of his uncle Kandinsky?[94] The name of the Schloss count was said to be

---

91 Beckett, *Stirrings Still*, in *The Complete Short Prose*, pp. 259–66.

92 Beckett, *Company*, p. 18.

93 Beckett, *Waiting for Godot*, p. 85.

94 It is perhaps necessary to reread Beckett's aforementioned 1929 essay, alongside Kojève's on Kandinsky from 1939 ['The Concrete Paintings of Kandinsky', translated as an appendix in Lisa Carol Florman's *Concerning the Spiritual and the Concrete in Kandinsky's Art* (Stanford, CA: Stanford University Press, 2014), pp. 149–74. —Trans.]. What remains to be painted after the 'spiritual'? Every possible 'case'—but precisely only 'cases'. The

Westwest. Is this a 'Name' to be interpreted like Godot? Does it not suggest the idea of that which endures in being, of an extremely firm existence? Everyone appears to believe so: Westwest is the highest entity, the immobile motor of the world-structure of the Schloss. At first, K. appears to ignore this, but immediately accepts this 'interpretation': it is Count Westwest who summoned him, it is to Him that one must turn for permission, it is He who dares to know (a brazen presumption, as the school mater admonishes).

Count Westwest would appear, then, to be the opposite of Godot. To the same extent that the latter is 'outside' the scene, the former 'informs' each movement, starting from K.'s very desire. And yet, in the end, neither the one nor the other is 'measurable'. Both names implode in inexhaustible waiting as such. 'They are' exclusively because waiting cannot be 'let go', cannot be 'de-cided', not even by hanging oneself. Hamlet's recital of suicide is accomplished in the concluding pantomime of *Waiting for Godot*.

No 'evidence' could 'convince' the acting of the Prince of Denmark. And yet he acts, ruthlessly. But he is only able to kill [*uccidere*], not to decide [*decidere*]. And if someone is destined to inherit the unhappy realm, it is that Fortinbras who seemed to constitute the most terrible threat: a promise of endless war, not of order and peace. Hamlet is action become stranger to itself; his past is *other*, and so is his destiny. Doing is nothing but *alienating oneself*— without a dialectic to reconcile oneself, without the balm of conciliation. In Beckett, the same situation assumes the irrevocable timbre

---

concept has been exhibited: art, Hegel *docet*, has become an art of reflection and mediation, produced by the mind. The 'cases' are all pre-judged in their essence, and if they wished to make themselves 'count', they could only appear *comical*. Would the only 'novelty' be found in declaring openly, *sine glossa*, this 'great Game'? Is this the current meridian of 'art', from Duchamp to . . . ?

of a crystal that has consumed all its light: the Other, if it is, is unable to reply, just as if it were not. Were it able to reply, its message would not arrive. Were it to arrive, there would be No One there to receive it. But this No One, as we have seen, is nevertheless 'something', and precisely the 'something' that feigns existence even after the last day, whose 'to do' is merely 'to act'—searching, questioning, waiting transformed into immobile recitation. This supreme fiction coincides with life.

In Beckett, this 'to act' manifests the end of dramatic form for a more substantive reason than the forgetting of the idea of the *zoon politikón*, which sustained the force of dialogic confrontation. Even the incommunicability of representation is incorporated into dramatic form, since it expresses nothing but the crisis of dialogue itself, its inability to 'conclude', while remaining within the ambit of its principle. Beckett's 'conversation', as in certain dialogues in *Ulysses*, does not stage a loss but a radical inessentialism: man is not a 'political animal'. And so, every *drama* must perforce become a priori impossible, because only for that being-there who, in its essence, is inter-est, is it possible to *do*.

But that is not enough. The classical dramatic form is grounded on one principle: that the suffering inevitably linked to existence (or rather: to wanting to be the path destined to us) finally leads to the *mathos*, to a 'clear' knowledge.[95] Being-there is *placed* en route, but only he can bring the path to completion [*perficerla*][96]—and it is this

---

95 *Pathei mathos*, 'learning through suffering', is a formula from Aeschylus' *Agamemnon* (lines 176–78). [Trans.]

96 It should be noted that, in Heidegger, being-there (*Dasein*) is not grammatically gendered, whereas Cacciari is using 'he', here, as the pronoun for a specific being-there who is en route. [Trans.]

capacity that can be learnt. This is a *terrible* teaching, because its essential content consists in knowing that precisely *tyche*—the case that strikes us to the point of destroying us—represents the sole *methodos* to know ourselves, to re-cognize ourselves as mortals who in anguish interrogate themselves on the possible conciliation between opposed domains of the divine. This is the essence of the *drama* that, in some way, Florensky was reminded of by *Hamlet*, the struggle between the ancient divinity of revenge and the 'unknown god'. And in the final scene, Horatio is assigned the task of drawing from this predicament a lesson.

All this has 'fallen away' in Beckett; everything is happenstance, as are Pozzo and Lucky; the past is rubbish, the future zero. There is no case to impart lessons any longer; suffering is just useless, that's all, whether it is 'adjudged' to be guilty or innocent. The *cure* that assails us when we find ourselves children of *tyche* no longer 'cures' anything; its form repeats itself in identical ways through different events. The path running between suffering and knowledge is inter-rupted, under that tree where the 'two' ('fallen' from where? when? why?) remain semi-paralysed, awaiting 'whatever' will continue not to come or for the strength to go, which they shall never have. It is the evidence of this situation, and the equally evident fact that their dialogue—in contrast to the dramatic one—is no longer in any way 'hunting' for a 'truth', that lie at the origin of the absolutely *comical* character that every work will have to assume after the last day.

How could an immobile adventure appear as anything other than comical? One in which thought becomes restive without being able to communicate, or expresses itself while confusing—as in Lucky's extraordinary monologue—barbarisms of sense with barbarisms of reflection? In which everything seems to have been decided, because nothing is left to be done, without anyone being able to decide any-thing? In which everything is *done*, and so the very meaning of the *drama* is lost? This situation, this world *must* appear irresistibly comical. No, it will no longer be possible to write both tragedies and comedies. The tragic Muse demanded that the catastrophe had meaning, and that the case we are involved in and in which we struggle could be recognized within a *mythos*, that it participate in a *common* destiny. But such a Muse was in essence akin to the ancient Thalia.[97] The laughter of comedy instructed the community as much as did the *threnos*, Melpomene's lament. Its *personae* were even more 'political' than the tragic ones. Already the Shakespearean 'fool' and clown teach us not only about the vanity of our projects, the pallor of our 'purposes', but also disabuse us of the idea that any lesson can be drawn from pain. Tragedy and comedy are given and taken away together. 'Inoperative' thought, doing reduced to waiting without decision, demands another scene. Kafka's 'parables', in the play of their infinite interpretations that fail to open up to any 'catharsis', indicate its necessity. Beckett 'realizes' it. I would not know how else to define it other than as 'the comic'.

In Hegel's great *Aesthetic*, this result was 'prophesied'. Indeed, it ends precisely with the examination of the comic form. Beckett is the true realization of those pages. Romantic irony, which posits and dissolves everything through the power of reflection, 'saving' that form of the I that constitutes its subject-*substratum* is not comic. Critique and the exercise of irony presuppose 'divine creative genius for which anything and everything is only an unsubstantial creature'.[98] Even less should one understand the comic as the expression of a noble spirit who judges the wretchedness of the world, despising and deriding it. That expression of will to power that intends to annihilate

97 Patroness of comedy in ancient Greek mythology, one of the nine Muses. Melpomene was the patronness of tragedy. [Trans.]
98 G. W. F. Hegel, *Aesthetics: Lectures on Fine Art*, VOL. 1 (T. M. Knox trans.) (Oxford: Oxford University Press, 1975), p. 66.

its object, without recognizing that its own subjectivity constitutes nothing but its other and inseparable pole, does not belong to the 'beauty' of laughter. All the forms of dissolving irony are under the sign of the 'accomplishment' of 'great form.' It is on the basis of this idea that Nietzsche thought he could still characterize great art as will to power. Instead, the comic is the word that works with its own impotence, action that knows itself to be immobile, thought that in thinking itself 'leads to contradiction and dissolves its own action'.[99] No god 'dictates' destiny, originating the *drama*; the subject 'suffers' it, but in the most violent contrast with its own self; action and thought cross and diverge, according to the most unpredictable combinations; the result is never in the hands of the one who has acted on the scene; thought as judgement reveals itself, ultimately, as 'out of use'; there is no other 'judgement' than the *process* itself, to which we are summoned by the simple fact of existing.[100] To judge would mean being able to 'accomplish'; but the *on attend*, the 'one waits,' does not permit completions. Or laments, since laments around its im-perfectibility would necessarily end up sounding like an accusation, or at least, would allude to other possible worlds. If I were to ironize, sarcastically or not, upon this world, I would, in any case, judge it against the standard of 'value' of an I who imagines being free of it or imagines being able to free itself from it, and who 'desperately' loves the idol of his own freedom. The comic dissolves this last dimension of the realm of images. It demonstrates its destiny: to

---

99 Translated directly from the Italian. The closest passage I've been able to locate in Hegel is: 'In comedy there comes before our contemplation, in the laughter in which the characters dissolve everything, including themselves, the victory of their own subjective personality which nevertheless persists self-assured'. *Aesthetics*, VOL. 2, p. 1199. [Trans.]

100 *Processo* means both 'process' and 'trial'; Kafka's book is translated into Italian as *Il Processo*. [Trans.]

be fictitious. Its laughter 'exhausts' the passion that is the last to die, love of oneself, *philautia, philopsichia*—without thereby wishing to 'judge' and without preaching new values that 'overcome' it. It does not judge and does not believe—not even that it is. The comic is the only radical figure of the *epoché*, of the 'suspension' of judgement.

When unhappiness can no longer be brought back to an 'order', and action manifests it as its own essence, it cannot express itself either in the form of tragedy nor in that of comedy. The latter always represents a determinate acting, even if one is deprived of all substance, and borne by a character that has lost its sense of belonging to an *ethos*. It is not a case of ironizing on this or that 'type', nor of investigating the reason for unhappiness and what it destines. Being unhappy has neither foundation nor justification. It manifests itself. No discourse could 'hide it' any longer. In the comic, its absence-presence appears naked. And only the comic can correspond to such unconcealment. It is the culmination of reflexive art, of the art that has sunk all 'beautiful' immediacy: it is precisely the unhappiness of being-there that *must* express itself in the form that appears to represent its negation. It is *logical* that it be like that. For it is the comical that is, in principle, *impotent* in *justifying* unhappiness. Its impotence describes its unrepresentability. You shall not make unto thee images of being unhappy, of its 'scandalousness'. 'Let it' be, without 'cursing it' with your 'understanding'. The comic, which seems to 'know' nothing of unhappiness (and even less of a *techne alypias*, an art of consoling), knows its unrepresentability—and this 'saves'.

The comic nature of works such as *Waiting for Godot* or *Endgame* permits a better understanding of why Kafka laughed on rereading his own 'parables'. Laughter will render justice to that unredeemable unhappiness which 'dissolves its own action' without any final saving theophany, but which is also able to *negate itself* as though it were a pale substitute for an impossible salvation. It is a fact that the condition of Nell and Nagg in their bins is immediately experienced as comic. But this is because nothing is 'added' to the naked presence of their being unhappy. Could one not instead *immediately* cry? Yes, but it would mean silence and nothing more, not the silence in which what is impossible in *discourse* is shown. To reach this result it is necessary to traverse the entire 'history' of contemporary art as a reflection, a mediation, a dissolving-analysis of the very world of representation, a self-ironic form and, finally, to laugh upon art's own impotence.

Unhappiness shows itself *sine glossa*. And the comic situation appears:

NELL: (*Without lowering her voice.*) Nothing is funnier than unhappiness, I grant you that. But—

NAGG: (*Shocked.*) Oh!

NELL: Yes, yes, it's the most comical thing in the world.[101]

It is ridiculous to aspire to place in an image, to define as a real possibility, the conciliation between idea and project, project and result, between action and the thought that claims to guide it, between that doing that is surviving in in-decision and the *drân* that is the name of the drama. Comic is what *remains* after tragedy, comedy and the innumerable ludicrous forms of their survival have reached the *bottom* of their own representative power. The supreme lie (that excessive falseness that Nietzsche denounced in Wagner) is to claim to be able to speak unhappiness via lamentation. It is only possible to show that we do not know its cause, to show it to be 'unjustified'. The comic *laughs* away all attempts to rationalize it, as it does all attempts to express it im-mediately. Only in comic form does all possible theodicy touch bottom.

---

101 Beckett, *Endgame*, p. 101.

Let's try to explain in the language of the Mystical[102] this paradox according to which that 'divine worth' (*Götter-Wert*) of lament, of which Goethe sings,[103] is eminently 'unable' to express happiness. How can we communicate the incommunicable in the most appropriate way? For Pseudo-Dionysus, the invisible Infinite can only be shown by *absolutely dissimilar* things. Those who maintain that one can approach suprasensible Reality via comparison, lie. The only true analogy is that which sheds light on the impossibility of all analogy. If I wanted to represent the suprasensible through sublime images, it would inevitably be as if I were seeking to make believe that its 'arcanum' could truly be understood in creaturely language. However, no one could be 'seduced' by an image *violently* dissonant with that of which it seeks to be an image. This is what happens when a celestial substance, the Angel, is represented in the form of a monstrous animal, or when we say that the divinity is a lion, or a ferocious she-bear, or even a worm. We are then pushed truly to imagine the absolute unattainability of the divine with respect to our imaginative capacity. Instead, to proclaim its beauty, its preciousness, to sing its praises by appealing to our human, all-too human virtues, or to the beauties of the world down here, generates illusions that can turn into guilty lies. Only the lowliest, the absolutely outcast, the stone discarded by all can, in their poverty, signal towards 'that' which is nothing other than *other* with respect to all possible definition.

Thus, the 'serious' lament misleads us about the radical unjustifiability and unfoundedness of the evil of being-there, precisely

102 This is likely an allusion to *das Mystische* in Wittgenstein's *Tractatus Logico-Philosophicus*, for instance, in its proposition 5.632: 'There is without a doubt an inexpressible; it shows itself, that is the mystical'. [Trans.]
103 Johann Wolfgang Goethe, 'Reconciliation' in *The Collected Works, Volume 1: Selected Poems* (Christopher Middleton ed.) (Princeton, NJ: Princeton University Press, 1994), p. 255 [translation modified].

because it claims to impose itself as the right[104] representation of it. The idea of unhappiness is saved in its most distant likeness, or rather: saved in what no one could confuse it with, in any sense, in what it even seems to negate. The laughter of the comic is this 'likeness'. It does not fall upon the impotence of determinate characters but belongs to the impotence that follows the exhaustion of the tidal wave of representations, analogies and narrations. It is laughter saturated in pure *aidós*, in shame and *pietas*, which *reflects* on the last day, on the sole 'art' that could follow from it; this is laughter which has *known* the end of tragic weeping *and* of comedy's irony. Leopardian *toto corde* [wholehearted] laughter: 'The more man grows [. . .] and by growing becomes more incapable of happiness, the more he becomes prone to and feels at home with laughter, and a stranger to tears.'[105] This laughter, in turn, is opposed to all sarcasm, disenchanted above all with respect to the 'power' of its own disillusion—since disenchantment changes nothing, in the same way that thought alone moves nothing. It safeguards the scandal of unhappy being from the recurring assault of ideologies, visions of the world, and secularized theodicies. It will only be 'permissible' to laugh at works such as those of Kafka and Beckett; only they *deserve* it.

Being-there speaks, it continues to act and to say. Being-there does not 'do' because it is sure of the answer or the result, but because it exists, always un-decided and in-complete—in the same way that words are not 'elegant symbols' to grasp reality, but *worlds* that open onto the abyss of the immemorial and on the unpredictable of the ever-future. With these words we must continue to allude to the

---

104 The word *giusto*, rather like the word 'right', can be understood in a veridical as well as a juridical and ethical sense. [Trans.]

105 Giacomo Leopardi, *Zibaldone* (Michael Caesar and Franco D'Intino eds) (New York: Farrar, Strauss & Giroux, 2013), § 4138.

unhappiness that shows itself. But, at this height of reflection, we can only do so through the means, the medium that appears maximally strange to its timbre. Beauty was unable to express divine substances; weeping cannot say hell.[106] The comic 'allows' itself to be shown. But what of divine substances? Does laughter count for them as well? Is the unhappiness that the comic 'saves' awaiting to imagine them in itself? Does Godot mean this as well? In the comic, absolutely 'poor' waiting, emptied of all meaning, appears to be the only one open to this possibility. Laughter finally silences all that which is not *deus patibilis* [suffering god], a stranger on earth, the son of a father to whom he will be unable to return and to whom he writes letters that will never reach their destination. There is no irony, no desacralization, no judgement able to touch this figure. And this shows itself in laughter, this most noble *facies*. In the laughter that empties, or that opens onto desire for the void, we encounter an invincible desire that tirelessly contradicts or un-says the 'folly for the need to seem to glimpse' (Beckett's 'testament').[107] Here and only here can the idea of the impossible happiness be safeguarded—here, inhaling this void, one can know (*sapēre*) its trace. The rest is unattainable Silence.

---

106 Implicit throughout this section is the central distinction from Wittgenstein's *Tractatus Logico-Philosophicus* between 'saying' [*Sagen*] and 'showing' [*Zeigen*], between that which can be spoken of and what cannot be spoken of but only shown. [Trans.]

107 Samuel Beckett, 'Comment dire' [originally published in *Libération*, 1 June 1989; now published along with its English version 'What is the Word' in *Collected Poems of Samuel Beckett* (Seán Lawlor and John Pilling eds) (London: Faber & Faber, 2012), pp. 226–29].

The Broken Parable [1]

Kafka's writing is certainly not metaphorical—nor allegorical. Should its shape be associated to that of the *parabola*?[2] For Przywara,[3] the parable is born of the *living likeness*, the likeness that becomes history, story, that risks itself beyond its own immediate meaning towards the controversial flame of interpretations, which is itself about to be *betrayed*. The authentic parable can never, 'in the end', re-converge towards its heart, its origin, and thus unveil its meaning.

---

1 Italian uses the same word, *parabola*, for both 'parable' and 'parabola'. [Trans.]

2 The use of the term 'parable' for Kafka is extremely widespread, but its meaning is hardly ever well defined (see Adorno, *Prisms*, p. 246). Consider the beautiful passage from Johannes Urzidil's *There Goes Kafka* (Harold A. Basilius trans.) (Detroit, MI: Wayne State University Press, 1968): 'The parable is a tremendous consternation, astonishment that there really are people [. . .] who without fear, reservation, or conscience dare to make a decision and carry it out' (p. 41). In other words, the parable invites us to take a decision in life that is de-viation [*s-viamento*]. The parable does not mask the unfoundedness of decision; all the same, it demands it, in contrast to ethical action which always pretends to *remain* on the well-founded earth, which it always has 'under its feet,' *iustissima tellus* ['most righteous earth'— Virgil, *Georgics* 2.460].

3 Erich Przywara, *Analogia Entis: Metaphysics: Original Structure and Universal Rhythm* (John R. Betz and David Bentley Hart trans) (Grand Rapids, MI: William B. Eerdmans Publishing Company, 2014 [1962]), p. 461.

The word re-*veals*.[4] In its word the 'original fire' can be sensed and endures but only inasmuch as it is re-*vealed*—and so is never in essence 'recoverable'. One can await it, nostalgically, but as one might the word that we always lack. The essential condition of the parable can be explained with the evangelic paradox: he who sees me (who listens to me, 'gathers' me up in themselves, 'reads' me) sees the Father (and thus the ultimate meaning lives in me), but no one has ever seen the Father. The parable retains its etymological value as juxtaposition, conjunction or comparison, but it does so by taking to extremes the dramatic asymmetry of its two dimensions. Whereas in the symbol it is the essential unity of the parts that must manifest itself *ictu oculi*,[5] in the parable it is the search for the 'right' image, for the 'right' trace or clue of meaning that comes to the fore.

The parable is essentially polyvalent. That distinguishes it *radicitus* [radically] from allegory as well, from the evangelical as from the rabbinical forms that demand *interpretive* listening. Who do you believe me to be? There is no *one* answer to silence further queries. The parable appeals to the utter *responsibility* of the one who has been 'summoned'. And yet, taken together, they form a *story* with a definitive meaning. Their whole form re-veals a message that, however problematic and paradoxical, indicates *a* path, an ultimate End. All parables can be interpreted as variations and approximations of the re-velation of such an End.

Kafka is the heir to this tradition, *beyond* its last day. The form of the parable spins within itself. It desperately seeks a way out, a passage, a path to the 'right' interpretation. All his stories are only

4 The Italian *rivelare* and *rivelazione* (which recur below) mean 'to reveal' and 'revelation', respectively. The hyphenation and italics again serve to highlight the etymology of the word, from the Latin *re*, 'to go behind', and *velo*, the 'veil'—to reveal as a going behind the veil. [Trans.]
5 In the blink of an eye. [Trans.]

ever parables. We can in turn *narrate* them—as in a sort of 'narrating theology' without God. Their bidding is persistent: try and tell us who we are, try to free us from our estrangement from ourselves. This is their intimate *provocation*, from which it is impossible to escape. But, equally, to which it is impossible to respond. The interpretation thus ends up being at one with the parable itself.

In the same way that Jesus' parables suffered the sad fate of allegorical interpretations, so too those of Kafka suffered from that of his 'friends', *in primis* Max Brod. But it is the fate of all 'churches', whether theological or literary, to de-construct the parables, reduce them to allegories or empty them in similitudes. 'Churches' are condemned to feign possessing the meaning that they proclaim.

The evangelical parable rings as follows: to whoever knocks, the door will be opened. Kafka's parable does not 'vulgarly' oppose to this faith the idea that nothing will open for anyone, that no one will ever be permitted to discover the origin, the meaning. Rather, it 'narrates' this question: what does 'open' mean? What does it mean 'to open'? What will be opened to the one who knocks? What will the one for whom it is opened be destined to discover?

To the importunate friend who insists on asking even in the heart of the night the following answer will be given: '*pulsate et aperietur vobis*' (Luke 11: 9).[6] But what does it mean that an answer 'shall be' given? What does this future mean? For it to be given tomorrow, the answer must already be here now. The door is already open. The friend must already have the bread we need, so as to offer it to us, whether forced or moved by our 'faith'. But if the door is open, if the bread is ready, why then do we not know how to enter, why can we not feed ourselves?

---

6 '[K]nock, and it shall be opened unto you'. [Trans.]

The son has returned. He recognizes from afar the father's farm: 'Smoke is rising from the chimney, coffee is being made for supper.' But he remains at a distance, in interminable attendance. He does not even dare to knock. The door is open; there is no prohibition. And yet he waits, and 'the longer one hesitates before the door, the more estranged one becomes'. But K. did not wait, he crossed the bridge, and yet he remained a stranger despite the fact that no barrier 'took'[7] the path from him. Why not cross the open doorway? Why return home in order to remain, as if impeded, at a distance? *Perhaps* an answer is to be found in the following questions: 'What would happen if someone were to open the door now and ask me a question? Would not I myself then behave like one who wants to keep his secret?'[8] To enter is to-be-interrogated. To enter is to be re-vealed. To be prepared for this *sacrifice*. Deciding to enter involves insisting on being interrogated, face-to-face with the stranger par excellence: oneself. We come to a halt on this threshold. Knock, it shall be opened to you. *Decide* then to enter. But know this: this is only the first of innumerable doors you will have to pass through. At each door, something will be asked of you. And no answer will be enough to 'give you peace'. One parable will be followed by another. Can you not bear this 'destiny'? Would you prefer that the door be bolted shut? Is that your *secret*?

The closed door is a reassuring image. The idol of the absolutely *Other*, with which to console one's impotence. In the hope that beyond the threshold there is an answer. Hoping that the answer awaits us, *beyond*. But the door is open and voices and messages from

---

7 The word here is again *tolto*, 'to take' but also often used to translate Hegel's *Aufheben* into Italian. [Trans.]

8 Kafka, 'Home-Coming' in *The Complete Stories* (Nahum N. Glatzer ed.) (New York: Schocken, 1971), pp. 445–46.

within can be heard continuously announcing that beyond *no* answer can be found, however much we may obstinately interrogate them as though they could be its revelation. In this way we survive, 'sheltered' from this error, from this image of Prohibition. But there is no Prohibition. The man from the country *decides*, '*entschliesst er sich*',[9] 'that it is better to wait until he gets permission to enter'.[10] He decides not to decide. He awaits a *guarantee*. K. does not remain immobile on the threshold; on the contrary, he asserts he wants to struggle, and yet for him as well the end remains that of obtaining *permission*.

If some 'power' lurking within were to have the authority to permit full access rights, it would necessarily be in close relation with the Law and would be able to explain its meaning to us. That's what we think. But nothing authorizes this thought. Permissions and prohibitions are interwoven in indecipherable ways, they cancel themselves in turn. No border is determined with the evidence that we require. From one room to the next, it is possible to pass thanks to the weakest of insistences. But the insistence of those who imagine that the answer should be torn from others, that the answer is in a place 'other' than the question, is simply the insistence of the one who has decided to wait. The man from the country *is* before the Law—and there he would remain, even through all the rooms and questions of all the guardians and the interrogations of all the Momuses. *Before* the Law, which is 'evident' in its unfoundedness. The man from the country hides from this unbearable evidence, exhausting himself in waiting for permission, in the same way as K. does in the 'fever' of his interpreting.

---

9 'He makes up his mind'. [Trans.]
10 Kafka, 'Before the Law' in *The Complete Stories*, p. 3.

Derrida has explained how the interdicted lies not between the man from the country and the Law—it is the Law. The Law is an 'interdicted space'.[11] You are never *within* the Law, but always in front of it—that is to say, *outside*-(the-)law.[12] The essence of the Law consists in judging; but to judge is to divide: *Ur-theil*,[13] an originary division that 'condemns' one always to divide. It is thus—supreme evidence. And with it we can proceed from room to room, from village to village, like the emperor's messages. If this going were not errancy, which is to say, if this going could conclude, in the end, by grasping the Law 'from behind', then our questioning, as it were, our search would appear as that which could *found* the Law itself, and hence there would no longer be any Law. The principle[14] of the Law goes deep once we no longer stand before it, once the *judged* becomes the judge. The *henosis* with the Law, or the intimate comprehension of its foundation, is impossible, in the same way that it is impossible to be at once subject and object, viewer and viewed.

In the beginning is the Word that decides and orders. Nothing can found it. We are in this evidence; in its Open we live, 'discussing'. In the Open, no closed doors are given; our gaze cannot bear its evidence. It enables us only to go on spying, persisting weakly, to

---

11 Jacques Derrida, *Before the Law: The Complete Text of Préjugés* (Sandra van Reenen and Jacques de Ville trans) (Minneapolis, MN: University of Minnesota Press, 2018), p. 51.

12 Cacciari writes *fuori*-legge which, unhyphenated, would be translated as 'outlaw'; the hyphenation emphasizes the being *outside* the law (in Italian the definite article—in this case it would be *la legge*—is implied) but sets aside the issue of criminality. [Trans.]

13 *Urteil*, in German, means 'to judge' (*Urtheil* is an archaic variant). The prefix *Ur-* means 'original' or even 'primeval', and is emphasized in Cacciari's hyphenation. [Trans.]

14 See p.1n2 in this volume. [Trans.]

delude ourselves as we await permissions and guarantees, cultivating our empty hope in messengers and intermediaries. And since it is in the Open that we live, without possible shelter, ontologically itinerant, no possible way out can be given to us.

The man from the country who *seems* to want to enter and the ex-ape in 'A Report to an Academy', who desperately seeks a way out, an *Ausweg*, express the same 'intention' from two different points of view. In the same way that the man from the country decides to wait, so for the ex-ape the way out ends up consisting of wanting to achieve 'the cultural level of an average European'.[15] The *imitatio hominis* to which the latter aspires will never be able to surpass the condition of motionless waiting of the man from the country.

But the ex-ape or neo-European protagonist of the most Leopardian of Kafka's writings exhibits a much greater awareness of his *analogon*, fixed before the Law, of the fundamental distinction that runs between being free and seeking a way out, a *Menschenausweg*, a human all-too-human escape route. The appeal for a way out calls for renouncing that *grosse Gefühl der Freiheit nach allen Seiten*,[16] that great, noble yearning towards a 'complete' freedom, which for Kafka coincides with the *indestructible* within us. But this yearning *knows* that there is no possibility for man to *choose* freedom, *die Freiheit zu wählen*.[17] In order to choose freedom, we would need already to be free. For us to want freedom, our will would already have to be unconditioned. The yearning for freedom *knows*, in contrast, that the will is conditioned on all sides. What we are able to want are only escape routes, to conform to the conditions of the already-condemned,[18] before the Law. But in addition to this knowing, it is

---

15 Kafka, 'A Report to an Academy' in *The Complete Stories*, p. 258.

16 That 'spacious feeling of freedom on all sides'. Kafka, 'A Report to an Academy', p. 253.

17 Freedom of choice. [Trans.]

inevitable that a thought should assail us: 'Had I been devoted to the aforementioned idea of freedom, I should certainly have preferred the deep sea to the way out that suggested itself in the heavy faces of these men'.[19]

The way out consists, then, in enclosing oneself again in the illusion of a 'safe' space—whereas the free being could only be given negatively, as in the desperate refusal to search for an escape route. In truth, we *remain* always 'out of here'.[20] No closed door can safeguard us; no obstacle can bestow upon us the 'spacious feeling of freedom'.[21]

The broken parable, a perennial source of misunderstandings. You seek out likenesses and comparisons, you call upon all sorts of 'support' for your idea, you attempt to make it chime with a story as a whole—and increasingly its meaning escapes you and its very form seems to un-make itself. And yet the parable is necessary. You would be unable to live without writing it. But the parable is a bridge, and where a bridge is suspended, without touching either one bank or other, the only path permitted is *aporia* and nothing more. We have called upon the help of *nomads* to save our city, but now they camp

---

18 'Already-condemned' translates *pregiudicato*, which means 'convicted criminal' as well as the 'prejudiced'. The hyphenation once again serves to bring the attention of the reader to the etymology of the word: *giudizio* meaning 'judgement'; 'pre-' implying having already been judged or condemned. Hence the standing before the Law as always already having been subjected to its judgement. [Trans.]

19 Kafka, 'A Report to an Academy', p. 255.

20 Kafka, 'The Departure' in *The Complete Stories*, p. 449.

21 This is analogous in Beckett (*Worstward Ho*): 'Know only no out of. No knowing how know only out of. Into only. [. . .] Whither once whence no return. [. . .] Beyondless. Thenceless there. Thitherless there. Thence-less thitherless there.' Beckett, *Nowhow On*, p. 104.

out in our squares, foul our streets and devour our animals. 'This is a misunderstanding of some kind; and it will be the ruin of us'.[22]

The misunderstanding is linked to the form of the parable; and it is only in parables that it is now possible to express oneself. But the parables now 'knock' on the Open. Their message sinks into the immemorable and the incomprehensible, just as the nearest village remains forever unreachable. Each word of theirs is 'between': separated from the origin, which it seems to have forgotten, as much as it is far from the goal, of which it presages nothing. The only way then (which is not the way to be free, perhaps not even the 'exit'), will consist in rendering the word clear, pure in its *indecision*, in its distance from all *sym-bolicness*, 'geometrically' sober and precise in its being-between.

We cannot think 'elsewhere' than in this language—which is in-comprehension,[23] a self-traducing consubstantial with the 'law' of the heterogenesis of ends that dominates action. Hence one can only 'narrate' in the form of parables. And since that is how we think, never will thought accept that we truly are. This language-logos does not in itself understand being, even less does it 'produce' it. It has its own reality inasmuch as it is 'elsewhere' than in life, inasmuch as 'away from here' is its only goal. This is what the 'literature' that follows the last day has demonstrated. Its word erases the illusion of its ontological relation to the thing; it de-realizes. It insists on the distance from any effective grasp of being, showing how we tirelessly

22 Kafka, 'An Old Manuscript' in *The Complete Stories*, p. 417.
23 The play on words here is untranslatable: *fraintendersi* is made up of the prefix *fra-*, meaning 'between', 'among', 'betwixt', and *intendersi*, from the infinitive of 'understand' *intendere*, and the suffix *-si* used with the infinitive to derive reflexive third person object forms. So *fraintendersi* means 'to misunderstand one another', with the hyphenation drawing attention to the between-ness of the understanding that is 'missed'—so to be *within* a relation of in-comprehension. [Trans.]

seek to be, while being unable to 'arrive'. This is the torment that the gods inflict on Kafka's Prometheus.

Kafka's project to unite in a single book *The Stoker*, *The Judgement* and *Metamorphosis* under the title *Die Söhne*, *The Sons*, is well known. This collection would have rendered immediately evident the ontological *insecuritas* of the figure of the son, the cardinal point of Kafka's parable. The son is the missing, the unrecognizable, the derailed. But he is also the *abandoner*. The father would, in any case, be unable to recognize him, because the son exists only to abandon him. He is not the victim of the father's incomprehension. Neither does he want or is able to 'occupy' the father's place. These 'psychological' readings of Kafka squander all his metaphysical significance. The son is 'simply' thrown out of the home and, even if he returns, he can only do so as a stranger. Whether he halts infinitely on the threshold, or whether he enters and is greeted as the prodigal son, he *is not* who he was at the time of the separation and abandonment, or of his exile. Which is to say, at the time in which he came to light as *liber*, as the son.[24]

No jealousy, no psychological conflict has led him to flee. Being-away, being-stranger is his name. He finds himself in the condition of K. at the start of the novel: an *abandoner* who cannot truly remember what he abandoned, who could not recognize it even if he were to crash into it. He can only look beyond, if he wishes to enact the re-*petition*[25] of that 'foundation of truth' from whence he comes. But since that foundation is inexpressible, he proceeds in the inexplicable.

---

24 *Liber* is Latin for 'free'; in ancient Rome, *liberi* was used to refer to children, offspring. [Trans.]

25 *Ripetere* is 'to repeat', which stems from the Latin *ri-* or *re-*, meaning 'once again', and *pètere*, meaning 'to go' or 'move towards', but that can also mean 'to ask' as in 'to petition'. [Trans.]

Let us imagine that the water in which Georg Bendemann[26] allows himself to fall is that of Lethe. And that it is from that water that the land surveyor K. reawakens.

---

26 The protagonist of Kafka's story 'The Judgement' (*Das Urteil*). [Trans.]

ADORNO, Theodor W. *Prisms* (Shierry Weber Nicholsen and Samuel Weber trans). Cambridge, MA: MIT Press, 1967.

———. 'Trying to Understand *Endgame*' in *Notes to Literature*, VOL. 1 (Shierry Weber Nicholsen trans.). New York: Columbia University Press, 1992.

ALBERTI, Leon Battista. *Momus* (Sarah Knight trans., Virginia Brown and Sarah Knight eds). Cambridge, MA: I Tatti Renaissance Library, 2003.

ALIGHIERI, Dante. *The Divine Comedy of Dante, Volume 1: Inferno* (Robert M. Durling trans. and ed.). Oxford: Oxford University Press, 1996.

———. *The Divine Comedy of Dante, Volume 2: Purgatorio* (Robert M. Durling trans. and ed.). Oxford: Oxford University Press, 2003.

ANDERS, Günther. 'Being Without Time: On Beckett's Play *Waiting for Godot*' in Martin Esslin (ed.), *Samuel Beckett: A Collection of Critical Essays*. Prentice-Hall, NJ: Englewood Cliffs, 1965.

ARISTOTLE. *Poetics* (Michelle Zerba and David Gorman trans and eds). New York: Norton & Company, 2018.

AUDEN, W. H. *Lectures on Shakespeare* (Arthur Kirsch ed.). Princeton, NJ: Princeton University Press, 2019.

BADALONI, Nicola. *Marxismo come storicismo*. Milan: Feltrinelli, 1975[1962].

BADIOU, Alain. *On Beckett* (Nina Power and Alberto Toscano trans and eds). Manchester: Clinamen Press, 2003.

BATAILLE, Georges. 'Molloy's Silence' in *On Beckett: Essays and Criticism* (S. E. Gontarski ed.). London: Anthem Press, 2014.

BECKETT, Samuel. 'Beckett: Moody Man of Letters'. *The New York Times*, 6 May 1956.

———. *The Complete Short Prose: 1929–1989* (S. E. Gontarski ed.). New York: Grove Press, 1995.

———. *Endgame* in *Complete Dramatic Works*. London: Faber and Faber, 1986.

———. 'Dante . . . Bruno. Vico . . Joyce' in Samuel Beckett et al., *James Joyce, Finnegans Wake—A Symposium: Our Exagmination Round his Factifcation for Incamination of Work in Progress*. Paris: Shakespeare & Co., 1929; New York: New Directions, 1972 [facsimile edn].

———. *In nessun modo ancora* (Gabriele Frasca trans. and ed.). Turin: Einaudi, 2008.

———. *Nohow On: Company, Ill Seen Ill Said, and Worstward Ho*. London: John Calder, 1992.

———. *The Unnamable*. New York: Grove Press, 1978.

———. 'What is the Word' in *Collected Poems of Samuel Beckett* (Seán Lawlor and John Pilling eds). London: Faber & Faber, 2012.

BENJAMIN, Walter, and Gershom Scholem. *The Correspondence of Walter Benjamin and Gershom Scholem 1932–1940* (Gershom Scholem ed., Gary Smith and Andre Lefevere trans). New York: Schocken Books, 1989.

———. 'On the Concept of History' (Harry Zohn trans.) in *Selected Writings, Volume 4: 1939–40* (Howard Eiland and Michael W. Jennings eds). Cambridge, MA: Belknap Press, 2003.

BLANCHOT, Maurice. 'Literature and the Right to Death' in *The Work of Fire* (Charlotte Mandel trans.). Stanford, CA: Stanford University Press, 1995.

———. *The Space of Literature* (Ann Smock trans.). Lincoln, NE: University of Nebraska Press, 1982.

BLOCH, Ernst. *Heritage of Our Times* (Neville and Stephen Plaice trans). Cambridge: Polity Press, 1991.

BONNEFOY, Yves. *Racconti in sogno* (Cesare Greppi trans.). Milan: Egea, 1992.

BRUNO, Giordano. *Cause, Principle and Unity, and Writings on Magic* (Richard J. Blackwell and Robert de Lucca trans and eds). Cambridge: Cambridge University Press, 1998.

CACCIARI, Massimo. 'Confrontation with Heidegger' (Timothy S. Murphy trans.). *Genre* 43(3–4) (2010): 353–68.

————. *Dell'Inizio*. Milan: Adelphi, 1990.

————. *Drân: Meridiens de la decisión dans la pensée contemporaine* (Michel Valensi trans.). París: L'Éclat, 1991.

————. *Icone della legge*. Milan: Adelphi, 1986.

————. Krisis. *Saggio sulla crisi del pensiero negativo da Nietzsche a Wittgenstein*. Milan: Feltrinelli, 1976.

————. *The Labour of Spirit* (Matteo Mandarini trans.). London: Seagull Books, forthcoming 2024.

————. 'Pensiero negativo e razionalizzazione. Problemi e funzione della critica al sistema dialettico' in *Pensiero negativo e razionalizzazione*. Venice: Marsilio, 1977.

————. *Saggio sulla crisi del pensiero negativo da Nietzsche a Wittgenstein*. Milan: Feltrinelli, 1976.

CELAN, Paul. 'Psalm' in *Selected Poems* (Michael Hamburger and Christopher Middleton trans). Harmondsworth: Penguin, 1995.

CIORAN, E. M. 'Beckett' in *Anathemas and Admirations* (Richard Howard trans.). New York: Arcade Publishing, 2012.

————. *The Trouble with Being Born* (Richard Howard trans.). New York: Arcade Publishing, 1976.

CURI, Umberto. *Meglio non essere nati*. Turin: Bollati Boringhieri, 2008.

DELEUZE, Gilles. 'The Exhausted' in *Essays Critical and Clinical* (Michael A. Greco and Daniel W. Smith trans). Minneapolis, MN: University of Minnesota Press, 1997.

DERRIDA, Jacques. *Before the Law: The Complete Text of Préjugés* (Sandra van Reenen and Jacques de Ville trans.). Minneapolis, MN: University of Minnesota Press, 2018.

FRANK, Manfred. *The Philosophical Foundations of German Romanticism* (Elizabeth Millán-Zaibert trans.). Albany, NY: SUNY Press.

FUSINI, Nadia. *B&B. Beckett & Bacon*. Milan: Garzanti, 1994.

———. *Donne fatali*. Roma: Bulzoni, 2005.

———. *La passione dell'origine: Studi sul tragico shakespeariano e il romanzesco moderno*. Bari: Dedalo, 1981.

GIRARD, René. *A Theatre of Envy*. Oxford: Oxford University Press, 1990.

GOETHE, J. W. 'Reconciliation' in *The Collected Works, Volume 1: Selected Poems* (Christopher Middleton ed.). Princeton, NJ: Princeton University Press, 1994.

———. *Wilhelm Meister's Apprenticeship and Travels*, VOL. 1 (Thomas Carlyle trans.). New York: A. L. Burt, 1839.

———. *Wilhelm Meister's Apprenticeship and Travels*, VOL. 2 (Thomas Carlyle trans.). London: Chapman and Hall, 1907.

HEGEL, G. W. F. *Aesthetics: Lectures on Fine Art*, VOL. 1 (T. M. Knox trans.). Oxford: Oxford University Press, 1975.

———. *Aesthetics: Lectures on Fine Art*, VOL. 2 (T. M. Knox trans.). Oxford: Oxford University Press, 1975.

———. *Elements of the Philosophy of Right* (H. B. Nisbet trans., Allen W. Wood ed.). Cambridge: Cambridge University Press, 1991.

———. *The Phenomenology of Spirit* (Terry Pinkard and Michael Baur trans and eds). Cambridge University Press: Cambridge, 2018.

HEIDEGGER, Martin. *Being and Time* (John Macquarrie & Edward Robinson trans). Oxford: Basil Blackwell, 1962.

————. 'The Thing' in *Poetry, Language, Thought* (Albert Hofstadter trans.). New York: Harper and Row, 1971.

HOFFMANN, Hasso. *Rappresentanza—rappresentazione: Parola e concetto dall'antichità all'Ottocento* (C. Tommasi trans.). Milan: Giuffrè, 2007.

————. *Repräsentation: Studien zur Wort- und Begriffsgeschichte von der Antike bis ins 19. Jahrhundert*. Berlin: Duncker und Humblot, 1974.

IDEL, Moshe. *Messianic Mystics*. New Haven, CT: Yale University Press, 1998.

JOYCE, James. *Finnegans Wake*. Oxford: Oxford University Press, 2012.

KAFKA, Franz. *Aphorisms* (Willa Muir, Edwin Muir and Michael Hofmann trans). New York: Shocken, 2015.

————. *The Blue Octavo Notebooks* (Ernst Kaiser and Eithne Wilkins trans, Max Brod ed.). Cambridge, MA: Exact Change, 1991.

————. *The Castle* (Anthea Bell trans.). Oxford University Press, 2009.

————. *The Complete Stories* (Willa Muir, Edwin Muir, Tania Stern and James Stern trans) (Nahum N. Glatzer ed.). New York: Schocken, 1971.

————. *The Great Wall of China* (Willa and Edwin Muir trans). New York: Schocken Books, 1970.

————. 'Fragments from Note-Books and Loose Pages' in *Wedding Preparations in the Country and Other Posthumous Prose Writings* (Ernst Kaiser and Eithne Wilkins trans). London: Secker and Warburg, 1954.

————. *A Hunger Artist and Other Stories* (Joyce Crick trans.). Oxford: Oxford University Press, 2012.

————. *The Zürau Aphorisms* (Michael Hoffman trans., Roberto Calasso ed.). London: Harvill Secker, 2006.

KOJÈVE, Alexandre. 'The Concrete Paintings of Kandinsky', Appendix to Lisa Carol Florman, *Concerning the Spiritual and the Concrete in Kandinsky's Art*. Stanford, CA: Stanford University Press, 2014.

———. 'Le concept et le temps'. *Deucalion* 5 (1955): 18–19.

KRIPPENDORFF, Ekkehart. *Politik in Shakespeares Dramen: Historien, Römerdramen, Tragödien*. Frankfurt: Suhrkamp, 1992.

———. *Shakespeare politico: Drammi storici, drammi romani, tragedie* (Robin Benatti and Francesca Materzanini trans). Rome: Fazi, 2005.

LEOPARDI, Giacomo. *Zibaldone* (Michael Caesar and Franco D'Intino eds). New York: Farrar, Strauss & Giroux, 2013.

NIETZSCHE, Friedrich. *Ecce Homo* in *The Anti-Christ, Ecce Home, Twilight of the Idols: And Other Writings* (Judith Norman trans., Aaron Ridley and Judith Norman eds). Cambridge: Cambridge University Press, 2005.

PRZYWARA, Erich. *Analogia Entis: Metaphysics: Original Structure and Universal Rhythm* (John R. Betz and David Bentley Hart trans). Grand Rapids, MI: William B. Eerdmans Publishing Company, 2014[1962].

SACERDOTI, Gilberto. *Sacrificio e sovranità: Teologia e politica nell'Europa di Shakespeare e Bruno*. Macerata: Quodlibet, 2016.

SALER, Benson. 'Religio and the Definition of Religion'. *Cultural Anthropology* 2(3) (1987): 395–99.

SCHMITT, Carl. *Glossario* (Petra Dal Santo ed.). Milan: Giuffrè, 2001.

———. *Hamlet or Hecuba: The Intrusion of Time into the Play* (David Pan and Jennifer R. Rust trans). New York: Telos Press, 2009.

SCHOPENHAUER, Arthur. *The World as Will and Representation*, VOL. 1 (Judith Norman, Alastair Welchman and Christopher Janaway trans and eds). Cambridge: Cambridge University Press, 2010.

———. *The World as Will and Representation*, VOL. 2 (Judith Norman, Alistair Welchman and Christopher Janaway trans and eds). Cambridge: Cambridge University Press, 2018.

SERPIERI, Alessandro. 'Il mistero del primo Amleto' in William Shakespeare, *Il primo Amleto* (A. Serpieri trans. and ed.). Venice: Marsilio, 1997.

SEVERINO, Emanuele. *Il nulla e la poesia*. Milan: Rizzoli, 1990.

SICARI, Antonio M. *Nel 'castello interiore' di santa Teresa d'Avila*. Milan: Jaca Book, 2006.

SUSMAN, Margarete. 'Früheste Deutung Franz Kafkas' in *Gestalten und Kriese*. Stuttgart-Kostanz: Diana Verlag, 1954.

SZONDI, Peter. *Theory of Modern Drama* (Michael Hays trans.). Minneapolis, MN: University of Minnesota Press, 1987.

TAGLIAFERRI, Aldo. 'Introduzione' to Samuel Beckett, *Trilogia* (Aldo Tagliaferri trans. and ed.). Turin: Einaudi, 1996.

URZIDIL, Johannes. *There Goes Kafka* (Harold A. Basilius trans.). Detroit, MI: Wayne State University Press, 1968.

VICO, Giambattista. *New Science* (Dave Marsh trans.). Harmondsworth: Penguin, 1999.